Children's Drawings
ICONIC CODING OF THE ENVIRONMENT

TOPICS IN CONTEMPORARY SEMIOTICS

Series Editors: Thomas A. Sebeok and Jean Umiker-Sebeok
Indiana University

Children's Drawings
ICONIC CODING OF
THE ENVIRONMENT

Martin Krampen

Board of Advisors
Deutsche Gesellschaft für Semiotik
Ulm, Federal Republic of Germany

Plenum Press • New York and London

Library of Congress Cataloging in Publication Data

Krampen, Martin, date
    Children's drawings: iconic coding of the environment / Martin Krampen.
        p.   cm. — (Topics in contemporary semiotics)
    Includes bibliographical references and index.
    ISBN 0-306-43647-7
    1. Children's drawings — Psychological aspects. 2. Semiotics. I. Title. II. Series.
BF723.D7K73 1991   90-25210
155.4'014 — dc20   CIP

ISBN 0-306-43647-7

© 1991 Plenum Press, New York
A Division of Plenum Publishing Corporation
233 Spring Street, New York, N.Y. 10013

Printed in the United States of America

Preface

This book is dedicated to all those who love children and their wonderful, often surprising, drawings. This means it addresses all those interested in their developing capacity to produce "iconic" signs: parents, teachers, child psychologists, artists, architects (since building drawings are treated here), and semioticians at large—to name but a few potential readers. Because of the broad audience, I tried to keep scientific jargon to a minimum. Whenever this was unavoidable, I tried to explain the terms in such a way that even beginners in psychology could understand my arguments.

I received the first impulse to think about a book like this from the International Year of the Child declared by the UN in 1979.

In a first phase of the project, I obtained drawings of the six different building types treated in this book from more than 100 children aged 3–12 years in Turkey during a stay there as part of the faculty of Architecture of the Karadeniz Technical University in Trabzon under the auspices of the UNESCO/UNDP program TUR/75/012.

My special thanks go to Dr. Erdem Aksoy, then president of the university, and Dr. Özgönül Aksoy, then dean of the faculty of Architecture and Civil Engineering, for their encouragement to carry out the project. I would also like to thank Dr. Kutzal Öztürk, Sevinc Ertürk, Ali Özbilen, Hasan Saltik, together with all the teachers in nursery and elementary schools in and around Trabzon who helped to collect the drawings.

In the second phase, drawings of the same building types were obtained from more than 100 children aged 3–12 years in the area of Schwäbisch Gmünd, southern Germany.

The drawings were collected by Stefan Blank, Theo Gonser, Joachim Hoff,

Inge Prestele, Jürgen Salver, Wolfgang Sattler, Klaus-Jürgen Schäfer, Jürgen Schmitt, and Ute Vollenweider, all students of the College of Design in Schwäbisch Gmünd.

A selection of both sets of drawings toured universities and schools in the Federal Republic of Germany in the form of an exhibition especially organized by Ingrid Lempp.

The main bulk of the work in coding the hundreds of building drawings was carried out by the author. He was helped considerably by Petra Brucker, who also contributed a set of drawings of the same six building types made by handicapped German children, most of them suffering from cerebral palsy.

Dr. Hartmut Espe, Walter Reimund, and Margarete Seiwert helped process the data. Sylvia Beamish, a "native speaker" of English, was my linguistic conscience.

The idea of "developmental semiotics" was triggered by the concepts of "adnormal" and "denormal" semiotics formulated by Thomas A. Sebeok. The idea was further debated and developed in many discussions with my friend and mentor Thure von Uexküll.

To all who helped with this book, but especially to the children who gave their drawings to the project, my sincere thanks.

Martin Krampen

Contents

vii

PART I

The Development of Intelligence and Drawing Ability in Children

Introduction

Some Problems concerning Children's Drawings

Where Do the Lines on Paper Come from?

Six-year-old Miriam is sitting with her crayons at the table. I ask her to draw a church. Without hesitation she starts drawing. After a few minutes she hands me her drawing and says, "Look, a church." The drawing shows a horizontal building with a gabled roof and four vertical windows. To the right of the building there is a steeple with a cross on top.

Where do these lines on paper come from? There is no church visible from the window. Nor does Miriam have a picture book with a church in front of her. Hence, her hand must have been guided from inside her body. From her brain? And if there was something like a church image in her brain—how did it get there? Supposing it has reached her brain from the outside world, why doesn't the church in the drawing look like the one in her neighborhood? These are some of the questions I want to tackle in this book.

This goal is best accomplished by treating the drawing as a complex sign that stands for something else. But this semiotic approach raises new questions: Does the drawing stand for the image in the brain or for a church in the environment?

Sign Processes

A semiotic account of how Miriam's drawing of the church came about is a complex story involving two halves of a complete sign process.

In semiotics, a sign process begins with a material entity that is present to an observer-interpreter in a channel. The channel may be addressing any given sensory modality or combination thereof. In the case of Miriam's drawing, she must have looked at several buildings that differed from others in that they combined a horizontal and a vertical element—a nave and a steeple. The former usually had vertical windows, the latter a cross on top. Miriam must have been struck by this combination. Thus she came to this as an element carrying a special meaning, which she interpreted as referring to all those buildings in her environment that presented such a particular combination of nave and steeple. In semiotics, the perceived meaning carrier is called a "signifier"; the meaning resulting from interpreting the signifier is called the "signified."

The first half of the sign process necessary to explain Miriam's drawing begins, therefore, with a striking difference in the built environment. This difference is transformed during perception into a meaning carrier (signifier) and an interpreting agency (interpretant) in Miriam's mind, giving it meaning (signified), that is, the specific name of a particular building type. This in turn refers back to any example of this building type in the environment (Figure 1.1).

This model represents so far the first half of a sign process that allowed Miriam to distinguish building combinations with a horizontal and a vertical element from other buildings in the environment. In semiotics this is referred to as the process of "signification."

The second half of the sign process is one of "communication." This presupposes the process of signification, or in this case that Miriam, via interpretation, has already established the connection between the signifier/combination of horizontal-vertical building element and the signified "building type

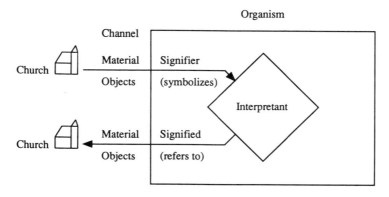

Figure 1.1. The first half of the sign process (signification).

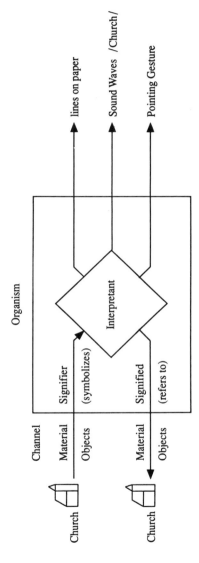

Figure 1.2. Model of complete sign processes (including communication) leading up to children's drawings.

church." She must also have acquired the name "church" for that unit of signifier and signified.

Thus my request has triggered a new part of the sign process via the acoustic channel and a corresponding interpretation. It starts in the interpreting agency, producing a disposition to make a drawing incorporating a combination of horizontal and vertical elements that finally issues in lines on paper. Of course, Miriam could have drawn a church without my request if, for example, she simply wanted to communicate to me what a church looks like. So my request is not a necessary part of the processes leading up to the drawing. Miriam could also have chosen to tell me what a church looks like. Were this the case, she would have used her vocal chords to produce air waves for the acoustic channel rather than her hand to draw lines on paper. Or she could have simply pointed toward a church during a walk, in which case she would not have communicated but displayed some instrumental behavior. In any event, the model of the sign processes leading up to Miriam's drawing can now be completed (Figure 1.2).

The Plan of This Book

Some Aims of This Book

One of the aims of this book is to clarify with the help of this model a complex interaction incorporating both semiotics and psychology. One term of this interaction is the "natural" development of children's ability to represent their environment (i.e., how the sign processes represented in the model are built up during infancy). The other term regards the emergence of a "cultural" and social content in the way in which children represent their environment. The questions I am raising here are what is nature (common to all children) and what is culture (common only to specific groups of children) in children's drawings.

The model (Figures 1.1 and 1.2) shows that what I have called the interpreting agency in the mind plays an important role in both halves of the sign process. In the signification process, it connects the signifier to the signified. In the communication process, it constitutes the source of drawing production. Is it possible to study the interpretant in the mind of children via the drawings originating in it? What is the nature of the interpretant? Is it a proposition of the kind "where there is smoke there is fire," that is, "wherever we have a combination of horizontal and vertical building parts, there we have a church"? Or is it an image conserving at least some topological aspects of the environmental object?

In this book I will compare evidence in support of both alternatives.

Studying the development of drawing ability and cultural influence in children's drawings finally amounts to an investigation of the development of the interpretant, that "central station" all sign processes have to pass.

A study of the development and role of the interpretant in sign processes is, however, too vast in scope to be dealt with here. Instead, I will limit the investigation to children's drawings of different building types, such as Miriam's church, the office building, the factory, the school, the apartment building, the house. I will be asking how these building types are differentiated in drawings on paper and, hence, in children's mental interpretations.

If the model is correct, children's drawings of building types connect, via the interpretant, back to the environment. Therefore, if these drawings incorporate aspects of the built environment they should also mirror—to some extent— its qualities or defects. Children's drawings have often been used to diagnose the developing personalities of their authors. But perhaps they may also serve one day as instruments for assessing the environment and help us to improve the quality of environmental planning both for children and adults.

Invitation on a Journey

The reader is now invited on a complex journey moving from general concepts to detailed data on several samples of drawings of buildings. This journey can also be imagined as a series of concentric circles that get smaller and smaller (Figure 1.3).

Since the development of sign processes in children has to be clarified, the journey starts at the periphery with what has been called developmental semiotics. At the beginning I will give a general idea of how different types of signs develop in children during their first and formative years. This will be followed by an account of the theory of Jean Piaget, the great Swiss psychologist and epistemologist who devoted his life work to the study of the unfolding sign processes in children. This first step also entails a discussion of terminology, comparing different traditions in semiotics.

Once a general idea of the development of sign processes has been provided, we will enter the second of the concentric circles to take a closer look at the development of imagination as put forward in Piaget's developmental scheme. Children's drawings, according to Piaget, constitute only one particular—albeit important—form of the imagination. In this context I will be confronting some arguments against the concept of the mental image and providing

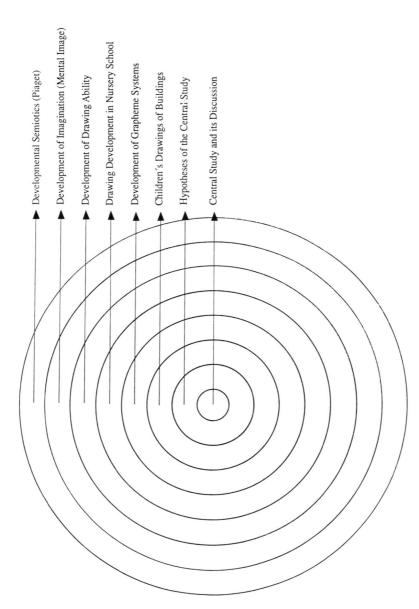

Figure 1.3. The plan of the book—a series of concentric circles with general theoretical issues at the periphery and a specific study on children's drawings of buildings at the center.

evidence in its favor. This will help to clarify questions concerning the nature of the interpretant in the child's mind.

Having confronted Piaget's definition of children's drawings as a phase in the development of imagination, the third leg of the journey will turn to major stages in drawing development.

The notion that children derive their drawings from "internal models" will prompt renewed consideration of the controversy surrounding the mental image and contribute to a more detailed description of the interpretant.

Moving further from the general to the particular, the fourth step will concentrate on the development of children's drawing activities in nursery school.

The fifth of the concentric circles leads to a still more microscopic scrutiny of "graphemes," the building blocks of children's drawings.

Since the way in which buildings are depicted in children's drawings is of particular concern to this book, the sixth step will consist in a review of early and more recent studies of drawings of buildings and building types done by children.

In the seventh circle I will take stock of what has been established regarding role developmental and environmental influences in children's drawings thus far in our journey. This inventory will lead to the hypotheses of the central study in this book.

That study and its methods and results will then be described in detail. Among other things, the latter will show the "developmental career" of six building types (office, factory, religious building, school, apartment building, and house) in drawings done by children between the ages of 3 and 12 from different cultures.

The book will conclude with a discussion of the results of this study. Two control studies to establish the ability of children to recognize building types from pictures are added to support the book's contention that drawings of buildings done by children originate from their mental image of the built environment.

CHAPTER *2*

Developmental Semiotics

The Subject Matter of Developmental Semiotics

A specific study of the development of children's drawings of buildings is more than an investigation into the development of drawings. If drawings are the result of sign processes, such a study also entails investigating the development of sign processes in general. I have called this overall investigation "developmental semiotics" in analogy to "developmental psychology," the study of psychological development of children (Krampen, 1981, 1986a).

Charles Morris (1964) had already hinted at a basic distinction in the development of signs when he distinguished between prelinguistic, linguistic, and postlinguistic signs. According to him,

> *prelinguistic* signs are those which occur in the child's behaviour before it speaks, or which later, even in the adult, are independent of language signs. *Linguistic* signs are those which occur in language, considered as a system of interpersonal signs restricted in their possibility of combination. *Postlinguistic* signs are signs which owe their signification to language but which are not themselves elements of language. The carved bear on a totem pole, the flag of a nation, the perception of a star as a large distant flaming object and the policeman's badge are examples of postlinguistic signs. (p. 58)

But it was only in 1975, at the first North American Semiotics Colloquium, that Thomas A. Sebeok called attention to the development of sign processes as such:

> Sign processes in everyday life, or the semiotics of the *normal*, need to be closely examined in the light of their ontogenetic formation, or the semiotics of the *adnormal;* their dissolution in the course of human life, or the semiotics of the *denormal;* and

11

their modifications when caused by injury or disease, or the semiotics of the *abnormal*. (p. 188)

According to Sebeok (1977), "two polar oppositions intersect here: one between the semiotics of ripening childhood and the semiotics of retrograde second childhood" (p. 188); the other between the semiotics of health and the semiotics of sickness. The specific merit of Sebeok's contribution consists not only in having introduced the topic of different phases in the development of sign processes, but in having extended its scope from the ontogenetic formation of sign systems in children to their dissolution during the process of aging—the latter phase constituting probably one of the most valuable research topics in anthroposemiotics for years to come.

Piaget's Theory of Mental Development

Piaget's Semiotic Theory

What is needed on the first leg of the journey is a theory explaining the development of all kinds of sign processes in children, that is, a theory of "developmental semiotics" in which the development of drawings may be embedded. The most comprehensive theory of this kind up to now is Piaget's theory of mental development in children (Krampen, 1981).

I will provide a broad outline of the general theory before examining it more specifically with reference to imagination and children's drawings.

Piaget describes mental development in four stages. The first is that of sensorimotor intelligence (up to 2 years). The second embraces the preoperatory representations (2–7 years). The third is the stage of concrete mental operations (7–11 years). The fourth is that of formal operations (11–15 years). The child's ability to represent his environment develops along these four stages.

Piaget's theory distinguishes clearly between the development of perception and perceptual activity (stage 1), imagination (stage 2), and conception (stages 3–4). For Piaget, perception is the sensory registration of static and object-centered spatial relationships, while perceptual activity is the active motoric search for a grasp of more complex relationships. Both belong to the stage of sensorimotor intelligence.

Imagination goes beyond perception and perceptual activity by internally imitating the apprehension of objects while they are out of sight. Imagination begins to develop during the initial "preoperatory" phase of the second stage. At first it is limited to the anticipation of concrete actions (stage 3). But finally it issues in free intellectual, internal operations on imagined objects.

The description of the interconnections and functional differences in the three developmental stages between (static) perception, perceptual activity, imagination, and the conception of concrete and formal operations requires a relatively complicated terminological apparatus. It is no wonder that Piaget found semiotics to be of assistance in generalizing his ideas into more universal terminology.

This semiotic terminology derives from the idea that a sign is considered a relational object. In semiotics, three sign relations are traditionally investigated:

1. The relationship of a sign to itself (i.e., the nature of its material structure, its color, etc).
2. The relationship to the object for which it stands (this object in most cases not being present—hence the use of signs).
3. The relationship between the sign itself, the object for which it stands, and the consciousness of the sign's interpreter (the "interpretant" binding together the sign and the object for which it stands).

The second of the three relationships has been proven to be of particular heuristic use in semiotic analysis. There are three possible kinds of relationships between the sign and the object for which it stands. These were first named by C. S. Peirce (1965, Book II, p. 143): iconic, indexical, and symbolic.

An *iconic* relationship is realized when the sign and the object have properties in common, as is the case in a realistic portrait of a person. An *indexical* relationship prevails if a sign becomes a sign only in temporal or spatial contact with its object, as in the case of the weather vane or the thermometer (the exception to the rule that the object is not present in the sign process). A *symbolic* relationship between the sign and its object, as in a person's name, is purely arbitrary, being based on convention and learning by its users.

It is important to realize that in this definition—in contrast to my proposed model (Figures 1.1 and 1.2)—no distinction is made between what I have called the "material entity" present to an observer-interpreter in a channel (for instance, a material sign) and the perceptual result of it (signifier), where the latter is then connected by the interpretant to the meaning (signified) which in turn refers back to material entities in the environment. This distinction between the material object external to the organism and the perceived object inside the organism (signifier) is also neglected by Piaget. In order to simplify matters, in the following pages the material sign/material object relationship will not be distinguished from the perceived sign/mental object relationship. Thus the sign/object and the signifier/signified relationship should be understood as including the external/internal and internal/external processes connecting organism and environment.

Piaget generalizes his findings on children's concept of space, sketching the development of the signifier/signified (sign/object) relationship. He follows this development from the early perceptual stage to mental representation by using images and concepts (Piaget & Inhelder, 1948/1967):

> Perception is the knowledge of objects resulting from direct contact with them. As against this, representation or imagination involves the evocation of objects in their absence or, when it runs parallel to perception, in their presence. It completes perceptual knowledge by reference to objects not actually perceived. . . .
>
> What is distinctive to representation is a system of meanings or significations embodying a distinction between that which signifies and that which is signified.
>
> Admittedly, perception itself contains significations (for example, forms seen in perspective are related to the constant form), but in this case they are merely signs or pointers, part and parcel of the sensorimotor scheme. In contrast to this, representational signification draws a clear distinction between the significants or signifiers which consist of signs (ordinary or mathematical language) and symbols (images, imitative gestures, sketches), and the things they signify (in the case of spatial representation: spatial transformations, spatial states, etc.). (p. 17)

Note that in this quotation the term *symbol*—used differently from the terminology proposed above—is identical with the term *icon*. I will come back to these terminological differences later. For the following discussion the reader should equate Piaget's term *symbol* with *icon*.

In the quote, several systematic distinctions are made. One is the distinction between perception, on the one hand, and imagination and conception, on the other. Perception is involved in the earlier phase of the signifier/signified (i.e., sign/object) relationship. Imagination and conception, together labeled "representation," imply two later stages of that relationship. The signifier/signified (sign/object) relationship thus evolves in three stages: perception, imagination, and conception.

In the first of these stages, that of perception and perceptual activity, the sense data are the signifiers, pointing to constant forms as their signifieds (Figure 2.1).

Thus a ball looked at from different angles is actually available as conical projection in the optic array to the retina. These sense data, however, are connected via the exploratory activity of perception to a system offering a series of conical projections through which a ball may be perceived. Whether these are large or small, all of them point to the constant form of an "ideal" sphere as their signified. Semiotically speaking, perception and perceptual activity serve the production of meaning by indexical signs (indices) based on present objects

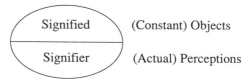

Figure 2.1. Indexical signs: perceptual data as signifiers and constant objects as signifieds.

and processes. In this stage of development, the sense data as signifiers are inseparable from the objects producing them and the signified object for which they stand.

The concept of the index as a semiotic function appears as early as 1936 in Piaget's *The Origins of Intelligence in the Child:*

> Concerning the "indication," this is the concrete signifier connected with direct perception and not with representation. In a general way we shall call indication every sensory impression or directly perceived quality whose signification (the signified) is an object of a sensorimotor scheme. In the strict and limited sense of the word, an indication is a perceptible fact which announces the presence of an object or the imminence of an event (the door which opens and announces a person). But as we have just seen, the concept of indication could be extended to include every sensori-motor assimilation. What I see of an inkwell or of a mountain is an indication of the existence of these objects; the rattle which the baby looks at is an indication of virtual prehension; the nipple which the nursling's lips touch is an indication of possible sucking, etc. The facts belonging to the present stage thus belong in the class of concrete significations of which the signifier is "indication." (Piaget, 1936/1963a, p. 191–192)

In the second stage of the signifier/signified (sign/object) relationship, described by Piaget as mental representation by imagination, the exploratory perceptual activity is internalized. The child now becomes capable of internally imitating the actions necessary to perceive an object from many points of view, without carrying them out externally. The result is what Piaget calls a symbolic representation in the form of a mental image. The signified of such a symbol is, for Piaget, the internal activity of imitation (without external gestures). Thus the child is—as it were—internally grasping an object, say, a ball, as if his hands were forming the shape of it. The result of imitating the roundness of the ball without actually carrying out the imitative action externally is a mental image of a ball.

While the signified is the activity of internal imitation, the signifier is the symbol, the image: the signified is the imitative action which has given rise to the image (Figure 2.2).

Signifier and signified are now distinct, albeit still "adherent" to each other. In perception, the sense data (as signifiers) were still an aspect of the

(Imitative) Actions

Mental Images
("Symbols")

Figure 2.2. Symbols (mental images, iconic signs): mental images as signifiers, imitative actions as signifieds.

signified. In comparison, the mental image as a signifier is now quite distinct from the imitative mental activities it signifies.

Semiotically speaking, imitation, imagination, and similar activities serve the production of meaning by "symbols" (i.e., images).

In the third stage of the signifier/signified (sign/object) relationship—called mental representation by conception in Piaget's writings—the symbol or image loses, to some degree, its importance. By now it is conventional signs (verbal and/or mathematical, according to Piaget) that constitute the signifier. The signifieds connected to these signifiers are internal thought operations on imagined objects (Figure 2.3).

These conceptual operations are, as a rule, directed toward forming classes of objects. In this case, mental images that have developed in the preceding stage play only an auxiliary role, for example, when a class of objects is imagined as a Venn diagram, or a series of numbers as a row of sticks or tallies. But at the same time, there are other mental operations aiming at the constitution of spatial or geometric systems. Each such system is like a single object, and it is a mental image that represents this object in terms of the operations that have constituted it. Thus, with the rise of conception, the two previous stages—perception and imagination—are not obsolete. They function on an equal footing with conception.

According to a suggestion by von Uexküll (personal communication, 1979), conceptual operations are comparable to what Freud called *Probehandlungen*. But they imply, in their final stage of development, a high degree of abstraction. You may experience these internal operations introspectively when you go through the advantages and disadvantages of choosing alternatives, such as deciding between various experimental designs before carrying out a research

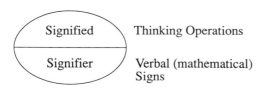

Thinking Operations

Verbal (mathematical) Signs

Figure 2.3. Conventional signs: verbal and/or mathematical signs as signifiers; thinking operation carried out on imagined objects as signifieds.

project. A case of conception involving symbolic representation occurs when you imagine various solutions for the plan of a house that you want to commission or to construct. However, the elements of these internal operations may also appear on more mundane occasions, for example, when you are planning the day's program or a shopping list.

Semiotically speaking, conceptual operations serve the production of meaning using signs. Sign and object are by now completely separated.

To summarize, the following signifier/signified (sign/object) relationships occur in the course of mental development in children. At the level of perception, the signifier consists of sense data constituted by different views of, or contacts with, the same object. The signified is the "constant object" seen from its various perspectives. At the level of imagination, the signifier is the symbolic representation of the mental image of an object. The signified is the internalized imitation of the perceptual activity necessary for grasping an object in its complexity. At the level of conception, the signifier is the sign, that is, the verbal or mathematical representation of objects or processes. The signified is the internal operation on symbolic objects constituted in classes or as spatial systems. At the conclusion of the stage of logical operations (about 14 years), the individual operates on all three levels—perception, imagination, and conception—with a dynamic interplay of all three faculties.

In *Psychologie de l'intelligence,* Piaget himself wrote the best summary of his theory of developmental semiotics, quoted here extensively in the English translation (Piaget, 1947/1963b):

> Direct observation of the child, as well as the analysis of certain speech disturbances shows that the use of a system of verbal signs depends on the exercise of a more general "symbolic function," characterized by the representation of reality through the medium of "significants," which are distinct from "significates."
>
> In fact, we should distinguish between symbols and signs on the one hand and indices or signals on the other. Not only all thought, but all cognitive and motor activity, from perception and habit to conceptual and reflective thought, consist in linking meanings. And all meaning implies a relation between a significant and a signified reality. But in the case of an index the significant constitutes a part or an objective aspect of the significate, or else it is linked to it by a causal relation; for the hunter tracks in the snow are an index of game, and for the infant the visible end of an almost completely hidden object is an index of its presence. Similarly, the signal, even when artificially produced by the experimenter, constitutes for the subject simply a partial aspect of the event that it heralds (in a conditioned response the signal is perceived as an objective antecedent). The symbol and the sign, on the other hand, imply a differentiation, from the point of view of the subject himself, between the significant and the significate; for a child playing at eating, a pebble representing a sweet is consciously recognized as that which symbolizes and the sweet as that which is symbolized; and when the same child, by "adherence to the sign," regards a name as inherent in the thing named, he nevertheless regards this name as a significant, as

though he sees it as a label attached in substance to the designated object. We may further specify that, according to a custom in linguistics which may usefully be employed in psychology, a symbol is defined as implying a bond of similarity between the significant and the significate, while the sign is "arbitrary" and of necessity based on convention. The sign thus cannot exist without social life, while the symbol may be formed by the individual in isolation (as in young children's play). Of course, symbols also may be socialized, a collective symbol being generally half sign and half symbol; on the other hand, a pure sign is always collective. (pp. 124–125)

Interestingly enough, the translators of this quote added the following footnote (Piaget, 1947/1963b):

This proposed terminology may conflict with existing usage in English. For example, C. R. Morris (in *Signs, Language and Behavior*, New York: Prentice Hall, 1946) uses symbol to mean any sign produced by an interpreter and acting as a substitute for another sign with which it is synonymous. All signs which are not symbols are signals. Morris's iconic signs and lansigns (or language-signs) appear to approximate to Piaget's symbols and signs respectively. (p. 125)

The truth is that Piaget's terminology does not "conflict with existing usage in English" but is derived from the "semiology" of the Genevean linguist Ferdinand de Saussure. His sign theory, which he called "semiology," arose independently of its American counterpart—"semiotics"—elaborated by Charles Sanders Peirce and later followed up by Charles Morris.

The Terminology of Peirce and Piaget

The two independent sign theories have generated conflicting terminologies, which may be clarified by the following equations:

(1)   de Saussure's and Piaget's "symbol" = Peirce's "icon"
(2)   Piaget's "index" = Peirce's "index"
(3)   de Saussure's and Piaget's "sign" = Peirce's "symbol"

Keeping these equations in mind, the reader can easily translate quotations from Piaget into Peircean terminology and vice versa.

Piaget knew Peirce's use of the trichotomy icon, index, and symbol but preferred to stick with de Saussure's conception, as becomes clear from the following passage in his *Structuralism* (1968/1971): "Must the symbolic function be thought of as permanent? Would it not be legitimate to think of what Saussure called the 'sign' as having evolved from what he called the 'symbol'?" (p. 114–115). And in a footnote Piaget continues:

Saussure's trichotomy strikes us as more profound than Peirce's. Saussure differentiates the index (casually connected with what it signifies) from the symbol ("motivated'') on the one hand and the sign (''arbitrary'') on the other; the sign is necessarily social, because conventional, whereas the symbol may be, as in dreams, individual. Peirce's symbol is an approximate match for Saussures sign, but it functions, not as a subdivision of ''representational signifiers,'' but as a contrast to icons (roughly, images) on the one hand, indices (roughly the same as Saussure's) on the other. (In other words, the contrast between pre-representational and representational signifiers and between individual and social signifiers does not enter Peirce's classification at all.) (p. 115)

There seems to be an asymmetry between Peirce's three sign/object relationships of icon, index, and symbol and Piaget's semiotic theory of the development of intelligence. For Peirce, the most ''primitive'' aspect of the relationship between the sign and the object it stands for is the iconic one, because similarity derives from overlapping properties between the sign and its object. For Piaget, however, this (partial) overlap or similarity between signifier and signified in the image already represents a step toward their final separation in concepts.

For Peirce, a less primitive aspect of the relationship between the material sign and the object it stands for is the indexical one, because sign and object have separate properties but, at the same time, are coupled by contiguity. For Piaget, on the other hand, it is the unavoidable link between signifier and signified object that is typical of perception. Contiguity makes perception a ''trap'' from which the child is liberated by the development of imagination and conceptualization.

The least primitive aspect of the relationship between sign and object in Peirce and of the signifer/signified relationship in Piaget is the ''conventional'' one. In this type of relationship there are no common properties nor necessary contiguity between the two terms. It is, therefore, considered the ''highest'' aspect of the sign/object relationship in Peirce. In this aspect he only differs from Piaget in terminology: Peirce calls *symbol* what Piaget calls *sign*.

In summary, Peirce's hierarchy of icon, index, and symbol taken as a sequence of ontogenetic steps in intellectual development stands in contradiction to Piaget for the first two terms.

The evidence of developmental psychology presented by Piaget is supported by Bruner's (1966) sequence of stages in the development of intelligence. Bruner calls the three successive stages the enactive, iconic, and symbolic phases. In the first, children know the world only through habitual actions. This presupposes, of course, an active and direct contact with the world (as in Piaget's perceptual exploration). In the second phase, a new form of representation is developed in the form of "imagery." Finally, actions and images become translated into language. According to Bruner, the three forms of representing the world leave important traces in the various phases of development. Their interplay remains one of the most important characteristics even in the intellectual life of adults, although different cultures may place different demands on the use of enactive, iconic, or symbolic representation. Even if Bruner's terminology is based on that of Peirce, his sequence of development resembles that of Piaget, with the indexical enactive phase preceding iconic representation.

My conclusion is to use Piaget's terminology for the purpose of this book. In this terminology, (motivated) symbols and images are equivalent to icons in Peirce's parlance. Hence I will use Peirce's term *icon* on equal footing with Piaget's *symbol* because it is plastic and unequivocal. Since the term *symbol* is occupied by Piaget to mean image or icon, I will use the term (conventional) *sign* whenever there is no "natural" bond between the sign material (or signifier) and the object it stands for, that is, its referent (or signified). This is the case, for instance, in verbal and mathematical signs.

CHAPTER 3

The Mental Image

The Development of the Mental Image

So far I have outlined Piaget's semiotic theory of mental development and have compared his terminology with that of Peirce. Now we are embarking on the second leg of the journey, where a more detailed account of Piaget's special developmental theory of imagination will be provided.

This step is necessary because for Piaget children's drawings constitute a special kind of imagination. Remember that for Piaget, symbolic and verbal signs are different from indexical ones in that they appear in the second developmental stage of intelligence. In that stage children begin to be capable of carrying out concrete mental operations. They do this by means of objects "conjured up" or represented in the mind that are not actually present in perception.

For a developmental semiotics of symbolic signs, Piaget's classification of symbols (i.e., icons in Peircean terminology) is of special interest because it, too, follows a developmental sequence as does his general classification of index, symbol, and sign. This classification is proposed in *The Psychology of the Infant* (Piaget & Inhelder, 1966/1969) in a chapter explicitly titled "Semiotic Function and Imitation." There are five classes of semiotic functions of imitation that develop successively. The first four concern "motivated" symbols, the last, arbitrary signs:

1. Delayed imitation (e.g., a child imitates the behavior of absent persons, such as the temper tantrum of a playmate hours after it has happened).
2. Symbolic play (e.g., a child mimics her own behavior; thus, when tired,

she may close her eyes, suck her thumb, and then put her teddy bear in a toy bed, making the latter a symbol of herself).

3. Drawing (in children's drawings, acquired graphic symbols—e.g., circles for a head, a ball, or a wheel—are used at first in the same way as toys in symbolic play, to assimilate, and later to accommodate reality).

4. Imagination proper (an object or a process is imitated internally without the appearance of outside gestures; the child accommodates herself to reality rather than assimilating it).

5. "Mentioning" (e.g., a child mews without a cat being present; the absent cat is verbally represented by arbitrary "signs").

From this classification it can be seen that children's drawings are considered a type of symbol appearing in the transition between symbolic play and imagination.

Piaget's theory on the stages of the development leading up to imagination proper forces a clear stance on what the nature of imagination is. This is tantamount to asking how environmental data are processed in the mind.

You will remember that in the model proposed at the beginning of the book the interpretant in the mind played the role of the "central station" through which connections between the signifier (the perceived object) and the signified (the meaning of this object) are made, and from which the processes leading to the disposition to execute a drawing and its terminal, the drawing, departs. In the following pages I propose a visit to this central station in order to gain an insight into how it functions. Of course, this talk about the central station is a metaphor. But in science the use of metaphors is widespread and unavoidable. I want to use this metaphor to lead up to the question, how are environmental data processed to issue in children's drawings? As far as Piaget's development of imagination by way of imitation is concerned, one metaphor that seems to impose itself strongly is that environmental data are processed in the mind as pictures. This brings us to the whole controversy of the "mental image" which I now want to face.

The Computer Metaphor versus the Picture Metaphor

The concept of the mental image central to Piaget's theory (e.g., Piaget & Inhelder, 1966) has not gone without criticism. One objection arises from the radical thesis that the notion of image is useless (or even confusing) as a theoretical construct for describing mental representation (Pylyshyn, 1973). According to this view, "what we know" is more adequately described as abstract conceptual and propositional structures to which we have no access in conscious experience. This type of mental representation is defined as "symbolic description" rather than image (where the term *symbolic* is used by Pylyshyn in the Peircean sense). Applying the imagery vocabulary, according to Pylyshyn, favors confusion since the picture metaphor suggests that the image is something to be perceived. Something to be perceived would require a "mind's eye." Instead of the image, Pylyshyn proposes what I call the computer metaphor.

Corresponding to the computer metaphor, Pylyshyn discusses three possible ways of representing knowledge in memory. One of these may be envisaged as a list of axiomatic propositions from which an unlimited number of hypotheses can be deduced (by thinking). These hypotheses function as questions to the knowledge system in the memory. A question posed to the knowledge system is transformed into a proposition to be proven within that system. A proof of the proposition (constructed by thinking) provides the answer.

Another kind of knowledge representation, according to Pylyshyn, could be conceived of as a data structure. Such a structure contains "symbols" that designate functionally important and invariant aspects of the environment being represented. They can be operated upon to represent other data structures in which, in turn, single symbols represent other data structures, etc. Data structures are often depicted as directed graphs, where the nodes represent symbols, and links designate various kinds of relationships.

The third type of knowledge representation mentioned by Pylyshyn is one in which concepts and facts are stored in terms of rules or procedures. What one "knows" after one has learned a concept is how it is used. Conceptual knowledge is, therefore, at least in part, a set of procedures for determining whether a particular token occurrence is an instance of a given concept, and a set of examples showing how to act with respect to the "known" fact. Procedural representations would not consist of propositions but of a hierarchical, goal-oriented, and partially ordered sequence of commands such as:

"If you want to prove that a given object is an x, then check first whether it has the property z by trying the following procedures . . . or, if they fail, by trying the following. . . . If any one succeeds proceed as follows. . . . If no one succeeds, try . . . etc."

After the discussion of these three potential types of knowledge representation based on the computer metaphor, Pylyshyn presents some speculations on what might be involved when the experience of visual images (which we all have!) occurs during a problem-solving process. In his view, interactions take place, during such experiences, between abstract concepts, like that of a number, and less abstract ones, like "my house." Since a considerable amount of "computation" is necessary during such interactions, the concepts involved must be kept available for access in some sort of "workspace." Activating a representation or "placing it into a workspace" functions like a deduction or construction of a more detailed representation than the cognitive task actually requires, and turns out to be picturelike. Pylyshyn writes about these "more detailed" representations:

> While picture-like entities are not stored in memory, they can be constructed during processing, used for making new interpretations (i.e., propositional representations) and then discarded. This approach views the content of the workspace as a model which satisfies the stored propositions . . . the model introduces no new information although it serves the invaluable function of making what was implicit in the description more explicit, accessible, and manipulable. (p. 19)

Picturelike entities then, according to Pylyshyn, are auxiliary ad hoc constructions that are more accessible than concepts and serve to "smoothen" the process of cognitive information processing.

It is remarkable that toward the end of his discussion, Pylyshyn is forced to reintroduce the image function that he so vigorously disavowed at the outset. He is forced to do so by the "dual-coding" evidence (e.g., Paivio, 1969, 1970; Paivio & Csapo, 1973; Ritchey, 1980) holding that coding of pictorial input in the mind is different from coding verbal material.

With respect to children, the evidence for dual coding, that is, one memory representation for pictures and another for words, is supported by an experiment carried out by Dilley and Paivio (1968). Children ranging from 4 to 6 years learned pairs of pictures of familiar objects and verbal designations in picture-picture, picture-word, word-picture, and word-word combinations. Dilley and Paivio found that pictures facilitated learning when they were stimuli (first item in the pair), but not when they were responses (second item in the pair). They interpreted this as a decoding problem at the mediating stage between pictorial input and verbal output. Pictures become a dead end in one modality, posing the problem of decoding an encoded picture into a verbal response. In an experiment carried out by Paivio and Yarmey (1966), this effect was more pronounced with children than with adults. This evidence cannot be dismissed by assuming that pictures and verbal labels activate a common, propositional "deep structure," as Norman and Rumelhart (1975) and Ritchey (1980) would have it.

To accommodate this empirical evidence on dual coding, Pylyshyn quotes Baylor (1972). Baylor proposes an information-processing model that features two separate but related knowledge systems in which information about the problem environment is represented. One system is called "S space" (for "symbolic," factual, and general information), the other "I space" (for imaginal and detailed information). The S space consists of a hierarchical data structure referring to more general and abstract aspects of objects and facts in a problem or task. The I space represents the more concrete spatial structure of integrated objects. The difference between the two forms of representation is that some information is represented directly in the I space that would have to be deduced indirectly in the S space. This means that the I space is more directly accessible. Baylor's saying that "visual mental imagery is just another representational system" is taken by Pylyshyn to mean that the mental representation corresponding to the image is like a description, and not like a picture. This would eliminate, according to Pylyshyn, the confusing reference to perception (by the mind's eye) connected to the notion of picture. Although not mentioning and obviously not familiar with the image concept of Piaget and Inhelder (1966), Pylyshyn seems, however, in accord with them in the notion that the mental image is no simple extension of perception.

What I wanted to show by reviewing an exponent of the computer metaphor is how difficult it is to replace the picture metaphor when dealing with the everyday experience of mental imagery, and the question whence it comes and how it is stored in the brain.

Research on the Mental Image in the USSR

Unexpected support for the developmental image theory presented by Piaget and Inhelder (1966) comes from psychological research on the image in the USSR (Vurpillot, 1976). A superficial look at Soviet research on the mental image results in the impression that the function of the image is to represent a faithful copy of the "real world." This interpretation of the image concept was rejected by Piaget and Inhelder (1966) in favor of the notion that the image constituted an assimilation rather than a copy. Apart from possible ideological reasons, however, the image theory, developed in its various aspects by Wekker (Vekker) (1966), Leontiev and Gippenreiter (1966), and Zaporozhets and Zinchenko (1966), was constructed with a view to guaranteeing successful practice in the real world: the image must represent the world in such a way that it constitutes an adequate basis for action. This requires a correspondence between the structure of stimulus properties and the structure of the subject's action potential. Only in this way can the reactions of the subject to the physical source of information be adequate. Therefore, the mental image must be the result of a translation into a code that preserves the structure of the spatiotemporal pattern present in the stimulus object. In other words, an image is a particular form of signal coding. How does this coding process operate?

According to Soviet psychologists, the stimuli issuing from their source undergo a first transformation in the receptors (Pavlov called them "peripheral analyzers"). They take on the form of neural excitations, that is, of signals in a frequency code. In this first transformation only a simple isomorphism is preserved between the source of stimulation and the subject organism. Next, at the level of the central nervous system ("cortical analyzers" in Pavlov's terminology), the simple frequency signals are transformed by various recoding operations into signal images containing a structure that is congruent with that of the stimulus source. According to Wekker (Vekker) (1966), only such an image—an iconic coding, as semioticians would say—can form the basis of an effective program for action. At the cortical level of neural connections, the range of movements that could be executed by the different effectors would be too large without such a restrictive basis. Only a coordination of the effector movements can reduce the degrees of freedom in the system in such a way that the effector movements in space will coincide with the physical structure of the source. It is an image that can best accomplish this reduction of degrees of freedom, because it conserves the geometry of the source of information. This role of the image presupposes a twofold coordination: one between the physical structure of the source-object and the geometry of the signal-image, and the other between this geometry and the structure of the movements controlled by it. In this way the response activity is integrated and adapted on the efferent side, because the perceived object is similar to the physical source object on the afferent side.

Most important for the purpose of this book on children's drawings are details on how perception of an object issues in the efferent action of drawing. Such details are given in an experiment by Vekker (Wekker) (1961). The subjects were asked to explore the contours of a small, relatively complex shape by hand and to draw the object under various conditions. The exploratory and the drawing movements were both filmed. A frame-by-frame analysis of the two kinds of movements showed that those made during exploration differed qualitatively in their whole structure from those made while drawing. For example, the exploratory movements were made in one direction along the contour, while the drawing movements proceeded in the opposite direction. The transformation of movement in time during exploration into a spatial image and the unfolding of the spatial image into the drawing movement in time is summarized by Vekker (Wekker) (1961) as follows:

> With unvarying handling movements, the movements realizing the drawing can vary in different respects: in point of departure, direction and speed for example. While in the process of formation of the image time-motor components pass into spatial components, different trajectories giving the same contour, in the process of regulation of

action by the image there takes place an unfolding of simultaneous-spatial components of reflection into time-motor components. *Contour* is unfolded as *trajectory*. And one and the same contour can unfold into a whole series of different trajectories, which are as it were contained within it in hidden form. (p. 139)

The process of signal transformation during perception is by no means conceived of as passive. It is rather regarded as "perceptive action" (Zaporozhets, 1965) also involving effector movements, such as hand movements while touching an object or eye movements following the outline of a figure.

If children's drawings issue from a mental image, how would this image be built up by perceptive action? Zinchenko *et al.* (1963) showed that there were differences between the perceptive actions of children when they "recognized" familiar objects and when they looked at unfamiliar ones. Two types of perceptive actions can therefore be distinguished—actions of recognition and actions of familiarization. In experiments using recordings of eye movements, Zinchenko *et al.* (1963) found that between 3 and 6 years of age the number of eye movements increased during the process of familiarization with a new object, whereas it decreased in the recognition of familiar ones. Such a result seems to indicate that the visual exploration of unknown objects becomes more intense, whereas the visual contact with known objects gets less intense with age. This could mean that the establishment of images is favored by intensifying exploration, while the recognition of objects is facilitated as images become consolidated. Some evidence for this hypothesis comes from another experiment of Zinchenko *et al.* (1963) in which they registered the eye movements of children instructed to imagine a form which had just been presented on a screen and then switched off. In children of 3 years there was almost no effort (in terms of eye movements) to imagine the form. This result appears to be similar to the condition in which their task was to get acquainted with an unfamiliar form. In contrast, children of 6 years showed an expanded eye movement trajectory almost as if they were "registering" contour and surface extension of the removed form. This was similar to their condition when asked to get acquainted with an unfamiliar form. Thus, both when getting acquainted with an unknown form and when using the imagination to reproduce a known form, eye movements get more frequent and correspond more to the contour and dimensions of the form as children grow older. In this sense the established image may be called a "motor copy."

In conclusion, it remains rather difficult to see crucial differences between the Soviet "motor copy" theory of the image and the theory of "active imitation" by Piaget and Inhelder (1966).

The Role of the Mental Image in the "Function Circle"

A first important point in the journey from the general theory of children's intellectual development to the study of their drawings has now been reached. I have examined evidence for and against the mental image as a possible mediator of actions, drawing included. No convincing argument has emerged against an iconic coding of the environment. The polemics against the mind's eye allegedly implied by the picture metaphor is easily refuted if the student of child development does not concentrate exclusively on the question of perception or storing incoming information, on the one hand, or on problems of action and production, on the other. All these processes must be seen together in a "function circle" (von Uexküll, 1921). Active perceptual search explores the environment. The image is an iconic coding device preserving important features of the stimulus sources in the environment in order to mediate successful action with respect to these. An image is built up first by perceptual contact with an object and continues to operate by internal imitation of perceptual motor activity when the object is out of sight. In fact, the image of an object is nothing to look at through a mind's eye; it is a *motor copy,* a topological template by which further action is controlled. The task of finding out how this motor copy is actually stored in the brain we will gladly leave to those who are interested in the computer metaphor or, better yet, to the neurophysiologists, who specialize in precisely this problem.

How the function cycle of children's drawings might work in detail was proposed for the limited case of copying and tracing geometrical figures based on a "closed-loop theory of perceptual-motor function" by Laszlo and Broderick (1985). Their model contains the following ingredients:

1. *Input*
   a. Information about environmental conditions (e.g., shape of the model to be copied = visual information)
   b. Body and limb posture (e.g., arm and hand positions perceived = kinaesthetic information)
   c. Instructions (e.g., "copy the model as seen from your position!" = acoustic, verbal information)
2. Central processes
   a. *Standard*
      —Memory traces of previous drawing attempts
      —Motivational processes
      —Plan of action (e.g., where to start the drawing, which direction to move in, how far to move before changing direction, how to achieve closure, etc.)

    b. *Motor programming unit*
       motor unit activation pattern to get arms and hands in the correct position (e.g., position of the resting hand holding the paper. For the drawing hand: positioning of the fingers and sufficient force to grasp the pencil, placing hand in starting position, defining the extent and direction of drawing movement, defining movement velocity, etc.)
3. *Output* (e.g., drawing)
4. *Feedback loops*
    a. Corollary discharge loop (e.g., intention to move) connecting motor programming unit (2b) to standard (2a)
    b. Secondary feedback loop (e.g., kinaesthetic and visual information about the progress of the movement, size and shape of the drawing, closure of the figure, force applied by the fingers on the pencil and the paper, movement speed, etc.) connecting the drawing action (3) to the standard (2a)

It seems that what is called "standard" in the central processes corresponds to the "internal model" of Luquet (1927) and to the "image" of Piaget and Inhelder (1966b). Semiotically speaking, the "interpretant" (standard) gives rise to a "disposition" to draw (motor programming unit).

CHAPTER 4

Drawing Development

The Empirical Study of Children's Drawings

History

By way of Piaget's general theory of semiotic development we arrived at his special theory of imitation. We found arguments for and against the "mental image" as a form of internalized imitation and representation. The evidence has led us to side with Piaget. For him, children's drawings were one particular form of imitation. With this in mind, the main topic of this book—children's drawings—is treated in detail in the third leg of our journey. First, however, I would like to present an historical survey on studies of children's drawings.

The psychological study of children's drawings can be traced back to a few pioneers (Cooke, 1885–1886; Hall, 1882/1892a; Perez, 1888; Ricci, 1887) who published on the topic in the 1880s, when psychology itself was still an infant science. These authors were struck by the spontaneous, sometimes contradictory look of these psychological documents.

During the last decade of the nineteenth century, the volume of publications on children's drawings increased considerably. Many aspects were treated by the authors which I will list here as completely as possible for readers with an historical interest (Baldwin, 1895; Barnes, 1893, 1894, 1897; Brown, 1897; Clark, 1897; Gallagher, 1897; Götze, 1898; Hall, 1892b; Hancock, 1894; Herrick, 1894; Hicks, 1893; Hogan, 1898; Lukens, 1897; Maitland, 1895, 1899; McDermott, 1897; O'Shea, 1894, 1897; Pappenheim, 1899; Passy, 1891; Scripture & Lyman, 1892–1893; Shinn, 1893; Sully, 1896; Tracy, 1899).

Research methods centered around surveys based on large samples (e.g., Barnes, 1893; Lukens, 1897; Maitland, 1895) or the comparative analysis of individual children's drawings (e.g., Brown, 1897; Lukens, 1897). Most studies were descriptive and answered such questions as "What do children like to draw?" (e.g., Gallagher, 1897; Lukens, 1897; Maitland, 1895). But the developmental problem of children's drawings also began to emerge. The first attempts to formulate stages of this development were made at the end of the last century (e.g., Lukens, 1897; Sully, 1896).

During the first decade of the twentieth century, more systematic surveys on children's drawings were carried out—even on an international basis (Ivanoff, 1909; Kerschensteiner, 1905; Levinstein, 1905; Stern, 1908). The developmental and ontogenetic variability of children's drawings became established (e.g., Burk, 1902; Stern, 1909). At the same time, studies on the drawings of individual children continued (e.g., Stern & Stern, 1910).

The second decade of the twentieth century was marked by a further elaboration of the stages in drawing development. Systematic comparisons of different methods of investigation were carried out during this period (Rouma, 1912), and the biographic method was perfected (e.g., Luquet, 1912, 1913). Drawing development was firmly established as part of the intellectual development of children (e.g., Rouma, 1912; Bühler, 1918/1932).

Consequently, in the second decade of the twentieth century, children's drawings became the object of psychometric testing (e.g., Burt, 1921; Gesell, 1925; Goodenough, 1926) and pedagogical concern (e.g., Muchow, 1925). Comprehensive books on children's drawings were published (Eng, 1931; Luquet, 1927). In a state-of-the-art report on the subject by Goodenough (1928), 110 studies are listed. By 1936, Graewe could compile a bibliography of 411 titles relevant to the study of children's drawings; later reports contain 330 (Goodenough & Harris, 1950) and 470 titles (Harris, 1963).

Methods

Regarding the above historical collection of studies from a methodological point of view, different positions may be distinguished. Barnes (1893) was the first to carry out larger-scale statistical surveys, whereas Luquet (1913) offered a qualitative method of direct observation on a single child's drawing development. He based it on more than 1,700 drawings produced by his daughter Simonne between the ages of 3 and 9. Rouma (1912) distinguished a number of methods, including methods of collection, survey, biography, direct observation, and some other methodological approaches to the investigation of children's drawings. Although in his first discussion on methods, Luquet (1922a) was critical with regard to the statistical method (cf. Luquet, 1924, and Lurçat, 1972–1973), he nevertheless admitted its advantages in testing hypotheses. Statistical studies may in turn be based on qualitative findings made during the longitudinal study of single cases. In fact, some important work on children's drawings was done by using both methods "in tandem" (e.g. Lurçat, 1979; Olivier, 1974).

In summary, the same contradiction between statistical and qualitative methods plaguing psychology in general can also be found in the study of children's drawings.

The Human Figure in Children's Drawings

One way of approaching the study of children's drawings is to limit the investigation to drawings of one topic only. Since I am going to limit my investigation to drawings of buildings, I thought the reader might appreciate a survey of other studies limited to single topics.

Studies of only one subject have been carried out on children's drawings of a chair (O'Shea, 1894), of animals (Graewe, 1935), of houses (e.g., Kerr, 1937; Markham, 1954), but mostly of human figures. This derives perhaps from the early finding that children like to draw human figures best (e.g., Gallagher, 1897; Maitland, 1895). As a result, it was soon discovered that drawings of human figures developed in a regular sequence from "tadpole men" to realistic representations. Thus, drawing stages were standardized (e.g., Gesell's Incomplete-Man Test of 1925), and finally, in 1926, the "Draw-a-Man Test" (Goodenough, 1926) was published as a diagnostic instrument for intelligence testing. The drawing of the human figure was scored on the presence (or absence) of limbs and other details, and the score was related to age (e.g., Golomb, 1973; Gridley, 1938). In several experiments external influences were isolated and controlled. Such variables were three dimensional versus two dimensional execution of the human figure (Golomb, 1974), the presence of human models, changes from two to three dimensions, changes in construction (Golomb, 1973), socioeconomic status, IQ, sex, and verbalization (Golomb, 1977). Familial retardates were compared with normal children (Golomb & Barr-Grossman, 1977). Even the influence of handwriting conventions (e.g., arabic right to left vs. left to right) on the drawings of human figures was studied (Denis, 1958). All these variables were found to have certain effects.

One book especially dedicated to children's drawings of the human figure (Meili-Dworetzki, 1957) emphasizes the influence of perception and gestalt on the drawings as opposed to the "intellectual" internal model (cf. also Golomb, 1973).

As with developmental studies on human figures, the investigation of animal drawings also yielded a consistent sequence (Graewe, 1935). At first, animals are rendered as humans and differentiated only by name. Later, animals are distinguished from humans by turning the human body horizontally. Distinctive features such as a tail or many legs are then added until such time as animals are given just four legs. Finally, the animal receives an animal outline from the start.

Cultural Influences on Children's Drawings

Since I have proposed analyzing natural and cultural influences in children's drawings, any summary of studies that failed to look at those concerned with the influence of culture on children's drawings would be incomplete.

Interest in the influence of different cultures on children's drawings began in the last decade of the nineteenth century, when McDermott (1897) published his article "Favourite Drawings of Indian Children" and Maitland (1899) wrote "Notes on Eskimo Drawings." The first decade of the twentieth century was characterized by large-scale international collections of children's drawings (cf. Levinstein, 1905). In 1930, Anna Schubert reported from the Institute of Educational Method and Practice in Moscow in her article "Drawings of Orotchen Children and Young People" (Schubert, 1930). The children of the Orotchen, a hunting tribe living in Siberia, drew good examples of naturalistic art similar to those of other hunting tribes in Asia, America, and other parts of the world. Their products resembled paleolithic cave drawings. The most amazing thing was that these children had not had any drawing practice and there was no figurative art in the Orotchen's cultural surroundings. The report concluded that the children's drawing process must have been based on outlining eidetic forms that were then projected onto paper and rendered with a pencil.

One study on human figures carried out in Egypt is of particular interest to this book. Wilson and Wilson (1984) investigated cultural influences in Egypt on children's drawings of human figures. Their hypotheses are formulated in analogy to Gombrich's (1969) contention that artistic images are modifications of conventional configurations shared by a group of artists. They also argued that children's drawings are not derived from their environment at large via imagination as the semiotic model and Piaget's theory would suggest, but from the stock of models and formulae present in the drawings of their peers. If this stock is limited, drawing development is restrained. If it is extensive, or if it can be supplemented from sources such as comic books or other media, drawing development would go further. Wilson and Wilson found that drawings of Egyptian village children differed from, and were less rich than, those of Egyptian city children, although there was evidence of a common Egyptian (or Moslem) style. For instance, both used arabic letters and numerals as schema for faces. Wilson and Wilson's conclusion that the course of development is determined primarily by "graphic models" (Wilson & Wilson, 1984, p. 25) needs confirmation from drawings on subjects other than the stereotyped human figure or even frequently drawn animals and the typical little house.

Piaget's Experimental Evidence

The study of children's drawings in terms of developmental semiotics became possible only after Piaget had elaborated his classification of symbols (icons), in which drawings were situated at a stage between symbolic play and imagination proper (see "The Development of the Mental Image" in Chapter 3, this volume). Since my approach is akin to Piaget's semiotic classification, his studies of and theories about children's drawings are of particular interest.

Piaget was, of course, very interested in children's drawings and published his own research on children's drawings of bicycles as early as 1922 (Piaget, 1922). He later returned to these drawings (Figure 4.1) in the chapter "Le

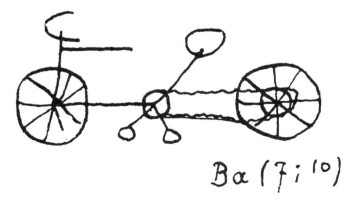

Figure 4.1. A child's drawing of a bicycle. From J. Piaget, 1927.

mechanisme des bicyclettes'' of his book *La causalité physique chez l'enfant* (Piaget, 1927).

A further important series of studies using, to a large extent, drawings as indicators of stages in the development of children's conception of space was published in *La representation de l'espace chez l'enfant* by Piaget and Inhelder (1948).

The original connection of symbols, in general, and drawings, in particular, with motor schemata as their signifieds is put forward impressively by one of the experiments in that book. In this experiment, children between the ages of $2\frac{1}{2}$ and 8 were asked to touch cutout geometric figures that were barred from sight by a screen. Later, they were asked to select the ones they touched from a whole group of other cutouts, or to draw them. The more the subjects were allowed to explore the contours of the shapes by touch, the better they were able to select or draw them. Thus the drawing appears to be one form of an iconic signifier. How should this signifier be connected to its signified? What is this signified? The connection must be the image that may be understood as a residue of the gestural motor activity in the nervous system. The signified must then be the tactile explorative movement that adapts to the shape of the form hidden from view. The sketch is, as it were, an imitative gesture leaving a trace on paper:

> The connections between image and movement seem quite clear. On the one hand there is a remarkably close correlation between the way the child explores the models he is given and his ability to draw them. On the other hand, the skill he shows in drawing roughly corresponds to his ability to recognize a shape by selecting it from a collection of visible models, though with simple recognition running ahead of drawing. (Piaget & Inhelder, 1948/1967, p. 41)

Another important experiment completed by Piaget and Inhelder (1948/1967) dealt with children's ability to copy geometric forms as an indication of their ability to handle spatial relationships. In this experiment children between the ages of 3 and 7 were given 21 different geometric shapes (Figure 4.2) as models.

Piaget and Inhelder found three different stages of development in the children's ability to copy these shapes.

Up to 3 years of age, children responded to the presentation of the model shapes by scribbling in purely rhythmical movement. However, in the first phase of the stage of concrete operations (Ia: up to 4 years), the scribbles started showing variations relating to the models. Distinctions between the copies of open (e.g., cross) and closed model forms (e.g., circle, ellipse, square, rectangle, triangle) became apparent. Subsequently (Ib: average age of 4 years), circles, squares, and triangles were copied as closed and round figures, while

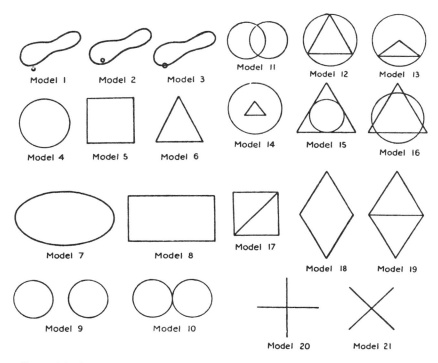

Figure 4.2. Geometric shapes used in a copying experiment by Piaget and Inhelder, 1948.

crosses were rendered distinctly as crosses. In other words, in this first phase, simple topological relationships such as inclusion, intersection, exclusion, openness, and closure were rendered. In the transition to the next phase, a distinction between round (circle, ellipse) and angular models (square, rectangle, triangle) was made, but not between the objects within these two groups (e.g., triangles were still rendered as squares). At the beginning of the next stage (IIa: above the age of 4), the copies took account of the number of angles and of the proportions of the models (e.g., triangle versus square or rectangle, circle versus ellipse). Smaller figures embedded in larger ones were now rendered correctly. However, their form of contact with the larger surrounding forms was not shown precisely (e.g., simple contact versus overlapping). Also, a simple rhombus could not yet be rendered. This form was mastered in the subsequent stage (IIb: up to $6\frac{1}{2}$ years), when the contact between embedded and surrounding form was also produced. At the level of concrete operations (III: $6\frac{1}{2}$–7 years), all 21 shapes were finally copied correctly.

On the whole, Piaget's studies on children's drawings impressively demonstrate the connection between touching and drawing [as in the drawing study of Vekker (Wekker), 1961] and the influence of age (maturation) on drawing ability.

The Influence of Luquet

Apart from his own studies on children's drawings, Piaget's theories closely followed the work of Luquet (1912, 1913, 1922a, 1922b, 1927), whom he quoted as early as 1923 (Piaget 1923a, 1923b). Based on his own studies of children's drawings, Luquet (1927) outlined a sequence of five phases in their development. Although these phases have met with criticism in some of their detail (e.g., Barrett and Light, 1976; Freeman, 1972), they still constitute an acceptable approximation to what can be observed in the development of children's drawings. Luquet's phases are:

- Scribbling (ages 2–3)
- Fortuitous realism (i.e., the discovery of similarities between certain features of scribbles and objects in reality) (ages 3–4)
- Failed realism (i.e., synthetic incapacity) (age 4–5)
- Intellectual realism (i.e., the child draws what she "knows" about reality, e.g., what is inside the house as well as its exterior) (ages 5–8)
- Visual realism (i.e., the child draws what is visible only from a certain point of view in reality, e.g., with a certain perspective) (ages 8–12)

Typical and most important in Luquet's scheme of phases (as opposed to proposals by other authors) is his basic hypothesis that behind the development of children's drawings there is a tendency toward realism. He devoted an entire chapter (titled "Le realisme") to this idea in his 1927 book *Le dessin enfantin*. In the end, the goal of drawing would be a realistic translation of the visual properties of objects into graphics. But according to Luquet (1913, 1927), children's drawings do not *directly* transmit the properties of objects. Children do not sit in front of objects copying them but, rather, put onto paper the properties of "internal models" of external objects.

Piaget's Three Phases in the Development of Children's Drawings

Considering his own interest in children's (nominal) realism and his concept of increasing accommodation to reality during the development of intelligence,

Piaget could not but sympathize with Luquet's ideas. In fact, Piaget and Inhelder (1948/1967) incorporated Luquet's phases into their own schemes of children's drawing development.

Piaget and Inhelder (1948/1967) describe three stages in the development of free drawing that appear very similar to those resulting from their experiment on copying geometric figures.

The first stage (I: up to the age of 4) is that of "synthetic incapacity." As soon as the child abandons his interest in observing the traces of his own motor activity left by rhythmic scribbling, he begins to take account of simple topological relationships in drawings, placing shapes close together that he associates in his mind (proximity) and separating them, if this is how he imagines them. Order is achieved to the degree of sequences of pairs. Drawing surrounding or enclosing forms is mastered as long as shapes are simple, but it still presents some difficulties when more complex forms are dealt with. Thus eyes may be placed outside the head, buttons outside the body. The roof may project into the house instead of skyward. At this stage the principles of continuity are dealt with only in a summary fashion. One of the principal indicators of synthetic incapacity is, in fact, that the parts of a figure are simply juxtaposed at their borderlines instead of being continuously linked together (e.g., an outline). This stage in free drawing is thus characterized by an unsystematic application of primitive topological relationships to complex shapes such as human figures, animals, and houses. The predominance of topological features that are not completely mastered is not due to a lack of drawing technique, but constitutes a law of development, as the experiment in copying simple geometric shapes has shown.

Following the stage of synthetic incapacity is that of "intellectual realism" (II: 4–8 years). Intellectual realism refers to the fact that children draw everything they know even if it is not actually visible from a certain vantage point. Topological relationships are completely acquired during this stage, whereas projective and metrical relationships (i.e., perspective and proportion) just begin to emerge without being coordinated. Proximities are correctly rendered: thus arms are attached to the trunk and eyes are placed side by side in the head (even if this is shown in profile). Order is present in the drawings of landscapes or houses, although not yet in accordance with the coordinates (e.g., the chimney is attached perpendicularly to the roof). Surrounding and enclosure become so important that in many instances the inside of an object (e.g., a house) is shown together with its surrounding outline in so-called transparencies. Some projective and metrical relationships of space are shown, but in an incoherent fashion. Since there is no coordination of viewpoints or perspectives, a single drawing in this phase presents many different viewpoints at once. This is also the reason for so-called pseudo-rotations, which show, for example, a cart head-on, the wheels attached in plan (circles), and the little man pushing it in profile—three different viewpoints at once! Straight lines and geometric shapes are used without regard to measurement and proportion. In a group of buildings, each may be shown from a different view. In intellectual realism, the elements of space just begin to become projective and metrical, but their relationships still obey the topological laws of proximity, separation, order, and continuity. Between the objects in space and the drawing there can be only an element-to-element correspondence of the features. But this correspondence is qualitative, and no coordination of the emerging projective or metric relationships can be seen. There is no understanding of perspective or proportion. No external horizontal or vertical coordinate systems combine perspectives and proportions into coherent wholes; hence, the result is a confused (though charming) medley of viewpoints.

In stage three (III: average ages 8–9), free drawings start to unite perspective, proportion, and distance. This stage is called "visual realism." Visual realism appears relatively late, since it requires the concepts of projective and metric space (perspective, proportion, metrical distance), which in turn presuppose advanced concrete mental operations. The projective and metrical concepts of space develop interdependently, and not one after the other. The projective relationships preserve the true relative position of shapes and figures as against the pseudo-perspectives and pseudo-rotations of intellectual realism. True proportions and relative or coordinate distances between shapes and figures are guaranteed by metrical relationships. Systems of mental operations merely replace empirical constructions.

By combining Piaget's and Luquet's phases, the following developmental sequence emerges:

- Scribbling (ages 2–3) is a late manifestation of sensorimotor intelligence.
- Fortuitous and failed realism is the same as Piaget's synthetic incapacity (ages 3–5) and is connected with the preoperational stage of mental development.
- Intellectual realism (ages 5–8) parallels the transition from the preoperational stage to the stage of concrete mental operations.
- Visual realism (ages 8–12) presupposes the developmental stage in concrete mental operations.

More recently the Piaget–Luquet phases of drawing development have been repeatedly criticized by a group of authors (Freeman & Cox, 1985) who, following Freeman (1980), like to engage in "Piaget-bashing," a term coined by Freeman himself (Freeman, 1980, p. 59), and, for that matter, in "Luquetbashing.'' These authors take a cognitivist stance and view the children draftsmen as ''problem solvers,'' ''strategists'' engaging in ''tactics,'' ''planners,'' and ''decision makers'' (e.g., Freeman, 1980, pp. 5, 33, 40, 80).

One particular technique used by them is coaxing children with increased contrast between objects and by guiding lines included in the models (e.g., Bayraktar, 1985) into earlier demonstrations of proneness in drawing performance than the Piaget–Luquet phases would predict. Allegedly, the little strategists know more than they are able to draw (because of production problems). The results of a dozen experiments (Freeman & Cox, 1985) are, however, generalizable at most to copying very simple geometrical figures.

"Internal Models"—A Special Case of the Image Controversy

Are Children's Drawings the Royal Road of Access to Internal Representations?

I have dealt at length with arguments for and against the mental image in general. After reviewing studies on children's drawings in general I now want to return to the mental image in connection with these drawings. Both Luquet and Piaget hold that, at least in the phase of intellectual realism, children ''draw what they know,'' putting certain properties of ''internal models'' on paper. It would appear that ''internal models'' are the same as mental images (or internal iconic representations). Can we presuppose that the state of children's drawings reflects the state of the ''internal models'' on which they are based?

There have been explicit warnings against regarding children's drawings as data of internal representation. Kosslyn, Heldmeyer, and Locklear (1977) conducted an experiment in two parts. In the first part, children in four different age groups (nursery school and grades 1, 3, and 6 of an elementary school) viewed different cardboard objects such as a cube, a prism, a house shape, etc. After looking at the objects, they selected drawings that they thought represented the shapes best. The selections were made from a set of drawings showing the objects in conventional, diagrammatic, symmetrical, and complex perspective, frontal elevation, and multiple elevations. In the second part of the experiment the children drew the same objects with the models present.

The experiment was obviously designed to detect discrepancies between the children's ability to select the best representation and their ability to draw. On the whole, the children preferred conventional perspective, but few of them drew it.

On the other hand, very few children preferred diagrammatic pictures (which showed the object parts in their interrelationships without regard to depth cues, occlusions, etc.), but many drew them.

It cannot be argued, however, that this disparity between preferences and drawings can establish whether preferences or drawings reflected the content of internal representation. In fact, the authors modestly conclude that drawings should not be taken as a "royal road" to the child's internal representation. But they do not exclude the possibility that internal representations play a role in determining the form of children's drawings:

> It has to be that internal representations are an important determinant of the child's drawing: he does not just draw randomly or independently of a model. Unfortunately, it seems exceedingly difficult to separate the possible influences of conventions (or lack thereof) from influences of internal representations. It seems reasonable to conclude, however, that children's drawings probably do not provide support for the view that the child's—let alone the adult's—representations in memory are like descriptions of an object's parts and their interrelationship. (Kosslyn *et al.*, 1977, p. 211)

Children's Drawings as a Problem of Production

The idea that children's drawings have little or nothing to do with internal representations is paralleled by a discussion on the discrepancy between (cognitive) competence and (drawing) performance that began at an early stage. Frances (1953), for example, found that children could "understand" perspective in paintings while they were unable to draw it. According to Goodnow (1977), drawing constitutes a problem-solving process for children—not a test of their knowledge. Freeman (1980) devoted an entire book to the analysis of those spatial skills and processes in children that sustain their "strategies" in "graphic problem solving." He is convinced that the old formula of "intellectual realism," namely, that "the child draws what he knows" should be changed to "the child knows more than he draws." In other words, easier tasks than drawings must be devised if we want to access children's knowledge. In shifting the focus of attention away from the mental image as a potential source of a drawing, Freeman instead emphasizes problems of planning a drawing (cf. Golomb & Farmer, 1983). He postulates decision models that are not only valid for different drawing tasks, but also more general actions. The more general models relate, for example, to the relationship children generally establish between the self and contextual cues in order to organize their actions. On the more specific level of drawing this boils down to asking which specific cues are used for orientation in the two-dimensional context of the drawing surface. Such cues could be, for example, the horizontal and vertical coordinates. These coordinates can be utilized for representing depth in a picture (e.g., "up on the page means further away"). In addition, Freeman gives some evidence of performance rules that help to solve compositional problems in free drawings. One such performance rule is the sequence in which the drawing of a human figure is spun off, starting with the head. Freeman (1980) is convinced that there is no privileged access to mental representation but that clearing away performance problems certainly would take us closer to the goal of describing representational structures in the mind.

That there are performance problems attached to drawing (depending on the age of the children) was shown by Piaget and Inhelder (1948) in the comparison between the forms children drew, and those they selected after they had been allowed to touch (but not see) them: simple recognition running ahead of drawing. But the evidence from Soviet studies on the gradual buildup of the mental image in children might also suggest that an as yet undifferentiated image can only yield an undifferentiated drawing.

Peculiarities in Children's Drawings Resulting from Undifferentiated Mental Images

The question of how faithfully children's drawings reproduce mental images was also approached in an experiment by Bassett (1977). Twenty-eight children with a mean age of 4 years were given the double tasks of drawing a man and constructing him from six cutout parts (head, trunk, two legs, two arms). Thus, the latter task removed the problem of drawing performance. The comparison between drawing and construction could theoretically yield two kinds of solutions, which in turn would yield two different interpretations:

1. The drawing could be as complete as the construction. In this case the child's internal representation could have been incomplete but could contain at least all the distinctive features of the human figure. Also, the children could have followed a Freeman (1988) type of production strategy if the serial and spatial ordering of the components were the same for drawing and construction.
2. The drawing could be less complete than the construction. In this case the child's internal representation could have been complete but undifferentiated. The cutout parts in the construction task would simply have furnished the children with a more differentiated picture than their mental image actually contained.

In Bassett's study, the serial order in which each child constructed the components (head, trunk, etc.) in both tasks was recorded. The result was that 24 out of the 28 children drew figures in which one or more of the components were left out, whereas all children constructed complete and correct human figures with the cutout parts as in case (2) above.

But in both tasks the serial order in which the components were drawn or constructed was the same. Most children started with the head and continued with the trunk or, in the drawings of tadpole men, with the legs, and added the arms after the legs. Since children could construct the human figure quite accurately with the cutout parts, their internal representation of it must have been complete. The fact that they followed a consistent serial order rules out any difficulties stemming from the lack of a production strategy. In conclusion, it can be inferred that the internal representation was complete but not clearly differentiated in its components.

Bassett (1977) concludes that there is evidence to suggest that the children "scanned" the internal representation of the human figure along a vertical axis from top to bottom. In the construction task in which differentiated parts were prepared for them, the whole figure was completed. Without this prepared differentiation some of the younger children rendered only the polar features top (head) and bottom (legs) in their drawings. Since lack of production rules does not seem to be the cause of this incompleteness, it can only be explained by inadequate image differentiation. In this respect the drawing of the tadpole man faithfully reflects an undifferentiated state of internal representation.

Internal Models and the Function Circle

To conclude this discussion on internal models we should once more note the danger of isolating the mental image from its afferent source and its efferent product. In the case of children's drawings it is particularly easy to be fascinated by the peculiarities of the signifier—the drawing on paper. From this fascination at the production end of the function circle (von Uexküll, 1921), researchers may be stimulated to a one-sided consideration of problem solving or production difficulties in children's drawings. While I do not maintain that the drawings have nothing to do with problem solving or algorithms of production, I refuse to isolate them from their remote origin in the actively explored environment. It is from the environment that the internal models on which the drawings are based are derived. Because these internal models are iconic codings of the environment, children's drawings are equally based on iconic codings of that environment, albeit one step removed. The function circle that leads to the production of children's drawings starts with the perceptual exploration of the environment and then leads, via the interpretant—that is, via the imitation of this exploratory activity in the internal model—to an internal disposition to make traces on paper controlled by that model.

In the process of communication these traces on paper become iconic signifiers for a perceiver who interprets them as referring back to the environment that was explored by the author of the drawing in the first place.

CHAPTER *5*

Drawing in Nursery School

Drawing and Writing

Piaget's general semiotic theory of mental development, his special theory of the development of symbolic (iconic) representation by images, and his detailed account on the development of children's drawings give a comprehensive framework to the present study. There are, however, some other specific aspects of the graphic activity of children that I would like to present in the fourth leg of the journey. These aspects are important because I have so far given little detail on the production end of the sign process involved in children's drawings. But without maturation of the peripheral muscular apparatus involved in drawing and its coordination with perception, the mental image could not be expressed on paper.

One particular aspect of sign production is the relationship between the development of drawing and writing, which was first studied in detail by the French psychologist Liliane Lurçat.

Starting in the late fifties, Wallon and Lurçat (1957, 1958, 1959) began to systematically investigate the development of children's graphic abilities in nursery school. This work was continued by Lurçat in the following two decades and summarized in her book *L'activité graphique a l'école maternelle* (Lurcat, 1979). The title of this book alone suggests that children's drawings—in the sense of iconic representations of objects and scenes—are seen as being part of a more general graphic activity comprising scribbling (early foreshadowings of writing) and the first attempts at drawing letters or writing. This approach has several interesting implications:

- It shows the common origin of images in drawing and signs in writing and how these two manifestations separate in the course of development.
- It points at the scholastic impact nursery school has on children (whether consciously produced or not); after all, this institution is called a school, not a *kindergarten* where children might grow like plants.
- It brings into focus two different functions that play an important part in the genesis of "visual literacy" (reading, writing, geometry, etc.): playful self-induced graphic exercises and an interest in copying, on the one hand, and graphic exercises and modeling directed by adults, on the other.
- It permits the derivation of modeling techniques carefully devised for pedagogical purposes and allows conclusions on possibilities and limits of pedagogical intervention.

Lurçat's work will be summarized by taking her three basic phases of graphic development in nursery school as a guideline and considering the development of the formal graphic elements, the figurative representations, and the attempts at lettering separately for each phase. For each of the three phases the capacity for expressing a mental image is inferred.

The First Phase (3–4 Years)

Formal Inventory

In the first phase of nursery school the children begin to abandon rapid motoric and unidirectional scribbling in favor of first curves, lines, and forms. In the course of time these take on the character of iconic signs, beginning with "ideograms" (take for instance the first "tadpole men"). Prerequisites for this development are two types of control, both consequences of muscular maturation (especially that of the flexor in the wrist): motor control and perceptual control.

Motor control leads to fragmentation of continuous lines by "breaking" rapid scribbling movements and to the rotative isolation of single lines out of tight scribbles.

Perceptual control can graft itself onto the slowing down and fragmentation of motor activity. Formerly, the eyes just followed the traces made by the pencil. Now perception of the beginning and the end of a trace allows the eye to control a "deliberate" return of the pencil to the beginning of the line just executed. From here the pencil may continue that line in another direction (simple control, Figure 5.1) or "close" an angle or a curve by a well-aimed trace connecting both ends

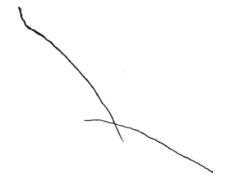

Figure 5.1. Simple control.

of a line (double control, Figure 5.2). It is interesting to note that the chimpanzee Congo, one of a number of "painting apes" that have been studied, was capable of double control (Figure 5.3; Morris, 1962).

The formal inventory, between 3 and 4 years of age, consists at the motoric level of curved open and closed lines (round forms) and continuous loops. At the level of perceptual control, circles, rectangles, spirals, hybrid slopes, arabesques, and crosses become possible. This inventory corresponds to stages Ia and Ib of the ability to copy forms in the Piaget and Inhelder (1948) experiment (see "Piaget's Experimental Evidence" in Chapter 4, this volume).

Figurative Inventory

First representations occur when the child gives a verbal name to the formal inventory's curves or shapes *before* they are drawn. Subsequently, the graphic forms of the inventory become ideograms of figural details (e.g., heads, arms,

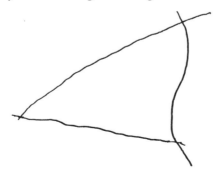

Figure 5.2. Double control.

Figure 5.3. A rare example of double control produced by Congo, a chimpanzee.

Figure 5.4. Examples of tadpole men.

Figure 5.5. Example of continuous hybrid slope.

Figure 5.6 Reversal of line direction produced by Congo, a chimpanzee.

legs, etc.) that are now verbally named *after* having been drawn. These details of whole figures are executed one after the other, each with its own graphic form, as if they were part of a list. Lurçat (1979) maintains that in this early phase each graphic form is an index of a detail in reality. Since these details must be known before they can be verbally enumerated, language continues to interplay with graphic activity. But it ceases to influence that activity totally as in the earlier stage, when names of objects are given to forms before drawing them.

Subsequently, graphic forms are used as schematic representations of whole objects (tadpole men, human figures with a trunk, animals, etc.) that again are verbally named (Figure 5.4).

Finally, whole ideographic objects are juxtaposed into scenes and interpreted by verbal enumeration.

In summary, during Lurçat's first phase the physical capacity to render mental images in drawings increases from ideograms over schematic representation to simple scenes.

Fundaments of Writing

During the first phase, the motoric preconditions of writing mature. As a result, antagonistic directions can now be controlled proprioceptively. This becomes evident in hybrid continuous slopes exhibiting reversals in the directions of wrist rotation (Figure 5.5). This control has also been observed in the drawings of the chimpanzee Congo (Figure 5.6).

The production of hybrids is, in fact, the motor base of writing. As yet, however, there is no differentiation between iconic and written conventional signs. It is toward the end of this development that children first imitate adults' writing or their signatures (Figure 5.7).

This leads to early attempts at "signing" their own drawings by hybrid slopes. Obviously, iconic and symbolic processes are still tightly connected.

Figure 5.7. Imitation of adults' writing.

The Second Phase (4–5 Years)

Formal Inventory of the Second Phase

In the second phase of graphic activity, the repertory of graphic forms expands considerably. This expansion is a consequence of further development of three kinds of abilities: motor abilities (e.g., the controlled combination of distal and proximal arm-wrist movements), perceptual abilities (e.g., visual identification of forms and identical reproduction of specific "geometric" forms), and representational abilities (figurative drawings).

Whereas the first phase was characterized by an oscillation between a priori and a posteriori verbal interpretation of impulsive graphic gestures and the repetition of simple schemata, graphic activity now becomes more organized.

The drawing surface is explored systematically in all directions. This leads to orthogonal realizations such as the following: vertical or horizontal lines and their combinations; parallels; rectangular grids and ladders (Figure 5.8); oblique realizations such as rays in different directions (Figure 5.9); curvilinear realizations such as elaborated arabesques (Figure 5.10).

Furthermore, orthogonal and oblique lines may be simply combined, or

Figure 5.8. Example of orthogonal realizations: a ladder.

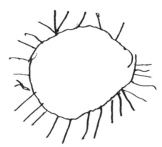

Figure 5.9. Example of oblique realizations: rays in different directions.

more decorative patterns are generated with oblique lines and arabesques. Finally, the drawing surface is organized in an even more complex and "intellectual" way. Symmetrical operations are tried outside the form, by juxtaposing it with the same graphic element (Figure 5.11), and inside the form by subdivision.

Parts of the subdivided forms are filled in with pencil or color. Forms are combined or laid out in a row and connected by a single dividing line. Parts of these subdivisions may again be filled in. At the end of this phase of development, we find large compositions that combine all the operations mentioned above: spatial factors such as directional lines; spatio-kinesthetic factors such as arabesques; and visual factors such as symmetry, subdivision, and filling in. All these operations work together in a highly decorative and aesthetic fashion.

This formal inventory of Lurçat's second phase is richer than that reported in Piaget and Inhelder's (1948) copying experiment for phase IIa, because copying a form does not take account of the ability to freely explore and subdivide a surface.

Figure 5.10. Example of curvilinear realizations: an arabesque.

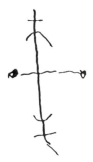

Figure 5.11. Example of symmetrical juxtaposition.

Figurative Inventory

In this phase, the represented object is "correctly" placed in the drawing surface (e.g., the human figure stands upright and "sleeps" horizontally). Formal exploration of the surface is also projected onto object representations. Figures are rendered in their conventional directions: front, back, above, below, vertical, oblique. Profile drawings appear, first in animals, later in humans. The concepts of opacity and transparency arise. Space is rendered within and between objects. Houses are first drawn as rectangles topped by a triangle (Figure 5.12). Later, figures are added within the rectangle (Figure 5.13). Finally, the rectangle is subdivided horizontally into stories and vertically into rooms that may each contain different objects (Figure 5.14).

"Outside" and "inside" are complemented by "above" and "below." The height and width of an object are drawn, but depth is indicated only by its opacity. There are still no attempts to render perspective.

Children pose their own themes. In the beginning, the events of the story unfolding in time are simply juxtaposed in space and connected by verbal comments. Later, an ad hoc connection is made graphically. For example, the arm of a human figure is elongated and attached by the hand to an object in order to show the action of grasping it (Figure 5.15), or persons and objects are included in a room.

The final step is the preplanned graphic connection of the elements of a story within a composition. Causal connections between objects are expressed through graphic connections that are planned in advance.

The ideographic scheme is abandoned in favor of more complex object representations. In their play with forms, children sometimes tend to get away from reality by stylizing and decorating the object, but they return to it in their representations. Thus there are, between the ages of 4 and 5 years, two opposing

Figure 5.12. The house first drawn as a rectangle topped by a triangle.

Figure 5.13. Human figure added within the house (transparency).

Figure 5.14. Horizontal and vertical subdivision of the house in stories and rooms (transparency).

Figure 5.15. The action of grasping represented by elongating the arm.

tendencies in graphic development; an abstract one in the progressive complication of forms and a concrete one in the tendency toward realism.

Lurçat's second phase corresponds nicely to Luquet's and Piaget's "intellectual realism," where children draw what they know according to internal models that are getting increasingly complex in a fascinating medley of viewpoints and transparencies.

Letter Drawing

During the second phase, nursery school teachers sometimes give the children letters to copy. A growing interest in copying generally develops at this age (4–5 years), and children often ask for examples to copy. Letter forms now also appear in spontaneous graphic activity and begin to replace hybrid slopes (Figure 5.16).

By imitating writing, the stock of forms is enlarged and changed. But the basic forms of letters, verticals and circles, often remain separated. If connected, they often appear in reverse order or mirrored in all directions. As yet, the writing is directionless, and letters "float" in the space given by the drawing sheet. Even in tracing-through exercises, the form of letters is not always respected. When copying letters and words from a model, children have difficulties in dividing their attention between the model and their own graphic realizations. But slowly, copies of visual models replace fantasy letters and slopes.

Figure 5.16. Letter forms in spontaneous graphic activity.

Single, printed letters are, of course, easier to copy than handwritten words. On the whole, whereas in the first phase the motoric basis of writing was established, in the second phase the acquired movements enter into conflict with the standard forms of the letters.

The Third Phase (5–6 Years)

Formal Inventory

In the last phase of nursery school, graphic activity is shaped by different competing influences. Thus, nursery school exercises also become visible in spontaneous drawings. The interests of the developing child's personality appear as drawings of individual fantasies and images. Consequently, there is a parallel tendency toward increasing graphic control and free graphic play, while the antagonism between abstract form and realism diminishes. The period between the ages of 5 and 6 is the ''age of the copy'' (Lurçat, 1979). Direct copying from examples of letters, shapes, and figures in nursery school has its repercussions in spontaneous graphic activity. External models are internalized and produced at will. Thus the stock of forms increases.

The previous conflict between abstract forms and realism in spontaneous drawings comes to an end because a certain inhibition in form production takes place. The forms produced are often minaturized or present the usual geometric shapes—circles, squares, triangles. Subdivision of these geometric shapes is further spontaneously exercised. The production of arabesques and cycloids is continued. The abstract tendency attached to the exploration of the drawing surface is now integrated with figurative drawing and is now expressed, for example, in the form of a highly decorated treatment of the human figure (Figure 5.17).

This formal inventory overlaps stages IIa and IIb of Piaget and Inhelder's (1948) copying experiment. But it appears to be more complex, since copying given examples is more limited than free drawing.

Figure 5.17. Example of highly decorative treatment of the human figure.

Figurative Inventory

In contrast to the formal inventory, the figurative inventory expands greatly. The number of represented objects is augmented, and objects themselves are differentiated. Instead of drawing just a bird, different species of birds are now represented. Aside from persons, the figurative inventory contains many kinds of plants (Figure 5.18), animals, and natural or human-made objects.

Verbal remarks describe or comment on the drawings *a posteriori*. The verbal comments may be realistic or playful. The human figure is rendered more realistically in its proportions and attitudes. The geometric decorativism of the previous phase becomes integrated into these figures as ornaments of their clothing. This increase of the figurative inventory during Lurçat's third phase should correspond to an increase in internal models resulting from a visual exploration of the environment. The tendency toward visual realism may be a consequence of sharpening mental images.

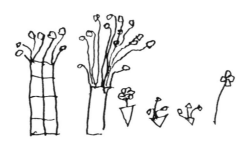

Figure 5.18. Different kinds of plants.

Figure 5.19. Examples of mistakes in the direction of writing.

Lettering Exercises

Whereas the second phase, with respect to writing, was characterized by a conflict between motoric tendencies and form control, in the third phase, letter forms are rendered correctly as a consequence of systematic learning. A lack of mastery concerning the direction of writing, however, persists. Mistakes in writing direction (Figure 5.19) are often compounded by the wrong sequence of letters.

When language is to be reproduced from a dictation, first graphic-phonetic connections are realized for well-known words, but generally the writing produced does not yet correspond to the meaning of the words. There are frequent inversions and orthographic mistakes. Thus, for example, Lurçat's subjects tended to use phonetic orthography for French words. In spontaneous writing, a playful treatment of letters is sometimes observed, as, for example, when the letter *o* is transformed by dots and lines into a face.

CHAPTER 6

Grapheme Development

General Hypothesis

Lurçat's work has provided a close look at the production end of children's drawings. In the fifth leg of our journey I will summarize studies made on an even more microscopic level on the elements of these drawings. This should clarify which restrictions are placed on the expression of mental images at which age.

For Lurçat, graphic activity is, at the outset, a unitary behavior that begins to split into two functions between the ages of 4 and 5: symbolic (iconic) representation and writing with conventional signs. Now I will present another French author, Olivier (1974), who goes one step further by asking the challenging question "Le dessin enfantin est-il une écriture?" (Is children's drawing a way of writing?). I would like to describe Olivier's work in some detail, since it is practically unknown in the Anglo-American literature up to this day (e.g., Freeman, 1980; Thomas & Silk, 1990; but see also Willats, 1985, p. 88).

The general hypothesis under which his research was conducted states that all children between the ages of 4 and 6 acquire the same quantatively limited stock of graphemes. These graphemes can be easily produced and combined. Like phonemes in language, they are meaningless in themselves; but during the phase of "intellectual realism" they are put together according to certain rules to form an unlimited number of meaningful drawings. Between the ages of 7 and 9, however, new rules begin to substitute for the preceding ones and the grapheme system dissolves to make room for other forms of graphic production.

This main hypothesis engenders three further complementary hypotheses:

61

1. Step by step the grapheme system should replace older forms of graphic behavior. The test of this hypothesis can be conducted by looking at changes in the formal inventory of children's drawings.
2. If the graphemes are only meaningless differential units being combined into meaningful wholes, children's drawings must be "doubly articulated" in meaningless and meaningful units like natural languages with their phonemes and monemes. This hypothesis can be tested by applying a graphic commutation test to children's drawings. This test would be analogous to the same test in language, where the commutation of phonemes, meaningless in themselves, alters the meaning of the morphemes formed by them (e.g., peer vs. beer).
3. Semiotically speaking, graphemes could have two functions. They could be either the signifiers of an original sign system in which signifiers and signifieds are mutually determined (as is the case in painting), or the signifiers of a substitutive sign system (as in the alphabet). Substitutive signifiers only replace original ones (e.g., speech sounds) that in turn stand in a rapport of mutual determination with their signifieds. In the latter case, the graphemes would merely serve, like letters, as substitutes for signifiers of verbally coded knowledge. This could be taken as one possible interpretation of Luquet's (1927) expression "intellectual realism."

In order to test these hypotheses, Olivier (1974) conducted two separate studies—one exclusively regarding the inventory of forms used in children's drawings, the other bearing on their content.

The research on forms consisted of a longitudinal study of his own three children, complemented by a quantitative test of its results with a sample of 180 nursery school children. The study bearing on content will be dealt with briefly after the research on forms has been summarized.

Inventory of Forms

Results of a Longitudinal Study on Three Children

First Tracings

Quite in accordance with Piaget and Inhelder (1948/1967) and Lurçat (1979), Olivier (1974) found a first differentiation of children's graphic activities during the second year of life: rapid and rhythmic rotative and hatched translative movements. By slowing down, miniaturizing, and fragmenting these two types of movements, two types of graphic traces are generated—continuous modulations of lines and discontinuous stereotyped graphemes.

Modulations (M)

Resulting from increasingly slow execution and better control of the first differentiation in rapid and continuous rotative or translative traces, three kinds of modulations become possible:

- Arabesquelike, predominantly rounding, continuous curves (Figure 6.1).
- Angular continuous traces (Figures 6.2 and 6.3).
- Modulations exhibiting both round and angular continuous traces (Figure 6.4).

First Grapheme System (G1)

Out of the modulations there emerges the first set of graphemes based on the slow execution and control of discontinuous traces. This is the result of the opposition of three pairs of distinctive features:

- Rotative (R) versus translative (T) traces
- Closed (C) versus open (O) traces
- Repeated alternation of line direction (rA) versus nonrepeated alternation (A)

The eight graphemes resulting from the combination of these distinctive features are given in Figures 6.5 and 6.6. These first graphemes may be combined in three modes:

- Intersection
- Inclusion
- Repetition

Figure 6.1. Arabesquelike, predominantly rounding, continuous curves.

Figure 6.2. Angular continuous traces.

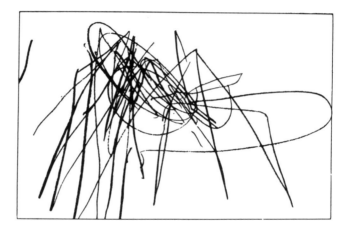

Figure 6.3. Angular continuous traces produced by Congo, a chimpanzee.

Figure 6.4. Modulations combining round and angular continuous traces.

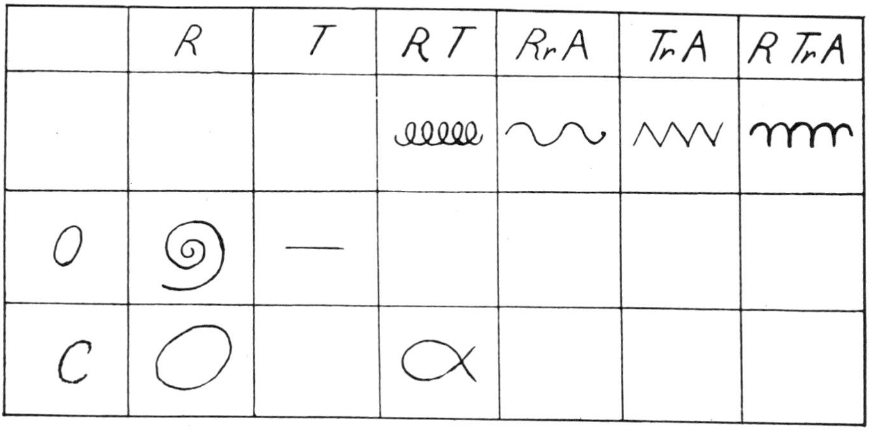

	R	T	$R\,T$	R_rA	T_rA	$R\,T_rA$
			ℓℓℓℓℓ	∿	∧∧∧	⋔⋔⋔
O	⊚	—				
C	○		∝			

Figure 6.5. The eight graphemes of system G1.

Second Grapheme System (G2)

The second set of graphemes is added to the first one by a new and distinctive feature that is a result of reducing the intersection of two graphemes to their controlled junction in one or more points. Thus the presence of junction (J) and the increased inhibition of repetition in alternation (A) differentiates between the eight additional graphemes and those of the first system (Figure 6.7).

The eight graphemes of the first and eight of the second system can now be further combined by the new mode of junction, together with intersection, inclusion, and repetition.

Figure 6.6. A zigzag drawn by Congo, a chimpanzee.

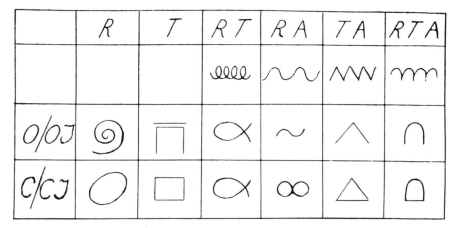

	R	T	RT	RA	TA	RTA
			ꬲꬲꬲꬲ	∿	⋀⋀⋁	⋯⋯
O/OJ	◎	⊓	∝	∼	⋀	∩
C/CJ	◯	▢	⋉	∞	△	⌂

Figure 6.7. The 16 graphemes of system G2, including eight of system G1 and eight new graphemes.

Third Grapheme System (G3)

The third set of graphemes is added to the previous stock by a new and distinctive feature resulting from the child's sensitivity to horizontal and vertical symmetry possibly related to the horizontal and vertical axes of the body. The forms thus acquire the feature of being symmetrical (S) around one, two, or three axes. Furthermore, another late distinctive feature appearing together with S seems to originate in a double alternation of an angle (aA), such as a diamond

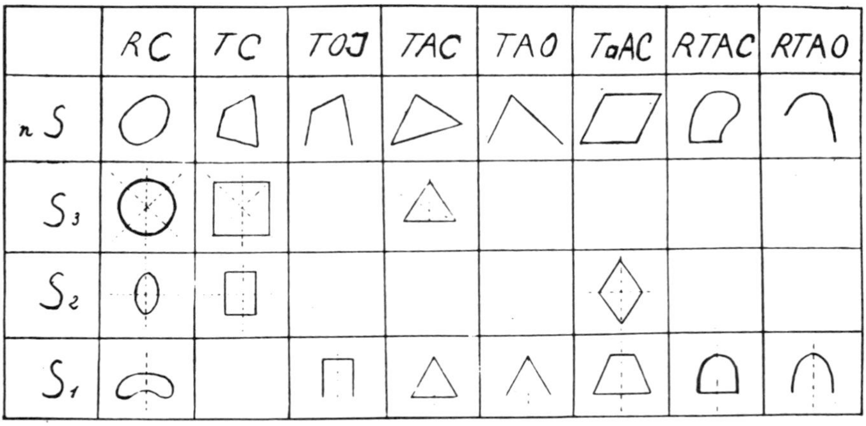

	RC	TC	TOJ	TAC	TAO	$TaAC$	$RTAC$	$RTAO$
$_nS$	◯	◁	⌓	◁	⋀	▱	⟁	⌐
S_3	⊙	⊡		△				
S_2	⏀	⊡				◇		
S_1	⇄		⊓	△	⋀	⏢	⌂	⌒

Figure 6.8. The 21 graphemes of system G3, including one of G1 and six of G2 (first row).

Table 6.1. Development of the Three Grapheme Systems in
the Longitudinal Study of One Child[a]

Age (yrs:mos)	Graphemes	Grapheme system	Mode of composition
2:9	○—〰	G1	Intersection, inclusion repetition
2:9–3:0	◎ ∞ ∽ □ ∩	G1, G2	Same as above + junction
3:0–3:3	〰 〰 ∧ △ ⌐ ◻	G1, G2	Same as for 2:9–3:0 age group
3:3–3:9	No new graphemes	G1, G2	Same for 3:0–3:3 age group
3:9–4:0	First symmetrical graphemes	G2, G3	Symmetrical juxtaposition

[a]From Olivier, 1974.

(TaAC). These two new distinctive features permit the differentiation of 14 more graphemes (Figure 6.8).

All 30 single graphemes from the three grapheme systems can now be combined by symmetrical juxtaposition in addition to the previous modes of intersection, inclusion, repetition, and junction. Thus, at the end of grapheme development, the nine aforementioned distinctive features (R, T, O, C, rA, A, J, S, aA) differentiate 30 graphemes that may be composed in five modes. The development of the three grapheme systems in the longitudinal study of one of Olivier's sons is shown in Table 6.1.

The Quantitative Control Test

Method

Subjects. Since the longitudinal grapheme study was based on qualitative observations of his own children, Olivier treated the results as a hypothesis to be statistically tested in quantitative investigations. The tests were administered to a total of 180 nursery school children of both sexes, divided into six age groups with a gap of half a year between each group starting with two pooled groups of 2:6–3:6 years and ending with 5:6–6:0 years.

Tests. First, the children were asked to execute a free drawing. Subsequently, they were asked to copy a selection of 14 graphemes. Finally, the children had to copy a drawing of a house that was composed of 10 graphemes.

Analysis of the Data. The data from the first free-drawing test were analyzed by counting separately the number of drawings containing at least one
modulation and/or symmetrical grapheme for each age group. If the results of the
longitudinal study were correct, modulations should decrease in the older age
groups and symmetrical graphemes should increase. In addition, the different
graphemes were assessed and counted for all age groups because the later grapheme systems (G2, G3) should appear in the older age groups but not in the
younger.

For the second test (copy of 14 graphemes), the number of correct copies of
closed graphemes (C) was compared with those of open (O) graphemes for each
age group to establish the sequence in which the opposition of C and O was
acquired in the grapheme systems G1 and G2. Correct copies of trapezoids and
parallelograms were listed separately to test whether they occur only in the older
age groups. Furthermore, the occurrence of round graphemes was compared with
the occurrence of angular ones, the presence of at least two angles in a grapheme
being expected to mark the transition from G1 to G2. Among the open forms, the
simple line (TO)—as opposed to the continuous slopes, waves, and zigzags—
was expected to be a criterion of G1.

The third test (copy of a house drawing) compared the house model containing 10 graphemes with the number of those correctly rendered in the copies by
the different age groups. It was expected that the number of correct copies would
increase with age. This comparison was limited to data from the two age groups
4:6–5:0 and 5:0–5:6 years.

Results of the Three Tests

The results of the free-drawing test show that the modulations continuously
diminished from age 2:6 (82%) to age 6:0 (25%). Conversely, symmetrical
graphemes augmented with age, but not in a linear fashion: they are not present
from ages 2:6 to 4:3. From ages 4:6 to 5:6 they reached their highest frequency
(74%), but a linear decrease began somewhat after this age to reach its lowest
level (50%) between the ages of 5:6 and 6:0 years.

This means that the free-drawing test generally confirmed the results of the
longitudinal study: the more primitive modulations disappear to make room for
graphemes. Symmetrical graphemes appear later in the development. What their
leveling off between the ages of 5 and 6 means is, however, not clear.

The results of the second test, in which the children were required to copy a
selection of 14 graphemes, show that the number of closed graphemes (C) that

are copied correctly rises from 1 to 4 in number as age increases. Whereas at the ages of 2:6 to 3:6 most children (53%) differentiated only one closed grapheme from the open ones, most children (93%) could distinguish four closed graphemes correctly at the ages of 5:0 to 5:6. The youngest group copied only one of the open forms (23%) of G1 correctly, but at the ages of 5:6 to 6:0 years, most of the children (72%) distinguished between all three repeatedly alternating (rA) forms of G1. Only 1–2 of the open forms of G2 (3–10%) were correctly copied in the youngest group, but all children between the ages of 5:6 and 6:0 could draw three of them. An increasing percentage of trapezoids (16–63%) and parallelograms (3–26%) were copied correctly only from ages 4:6 to 6:0.

These results not only confirm the results of Olivier's longitudinal study but are also in keeping with Piaget and Inhelder's (1948/1967) copying study. Here we must bear in mind that closed forms require quite difficult perceptual-motor coordination, since the hand has to lead the pencil exactly to the beginning of the line which has been drawn.

The third test, copying a house composed of 10 graphemes, showed results similar to the second test. Whereas most children between 4:6 and 5:0 years rendered only 2–3 closed and 1–2 of the two repeatedly alternating forms, most of them (95%) differentiated between the four repeatedly alternating forms at ages 5:0 to 5:6. This test again confirms the results of Olivier's longitudinal study.

Summary of the Test Results

In summarizing the results of the three tests, it has been found that Olivier's hypotheses could be confirmed, at least in their outline. The progressive disappearance of modulations with age confirms the first supplementary hypothesis of Olivier's (1974) study: An "older" graphic behavior, modulation, is slowly replaced by a new one, the production of graphemes. For the purposes of my own study, this suggests that children have little or no production capacity at their disposal during the phase of modulation for expressing the configurations of mental images. The strongest drop in modulations occurs only at the end of the 5th year, when the children reach their peak (93%) in differentiating between four closed symmetrical graphemes. The strong increase (from 0 to 73%) in the symmetrical graphemes of the free drawings occurs at 4:0 to 4:6 years, when 43% of the children differentiate correctly between the three closed forms of test 2. It is at this age, when all five modes of composition are present, that the children can begin to acquire grapheme system G3. With this production capacity it can also be expected that interesting renderings of the configurations of mental images are now possible.

Study of Content Relationships

Commutation Test with Graphemes

Up to now I have only reviewed the evidence on an increase in graphemes considered to be the formal building blocks of children's drawings. But so far the question as to how formal units (signifiers) are connected to the content they transmit (signified) remains open. Remember that Olivier's (1974) second supplementary hypothesis refers to the question of whether children's drawings might be doubly articulated in meaningful units (morphemes) composed in turn of merely differential but otherwise meaningless units (graphemes). An examination of children's drawings will show that in contrast to language, where phonemes remain mere differentiating units, graphemes may acquire the status of morphemes in the context of other graphemes. Thus it is true that the round (RC) is in itself a minimal differentiating element, as is the line (TO). But in combination with other rounds and lines, they may make up meaningful units such as the head, eyes, body, legs, arms, mouth, and nose. But these meanings do not seem to be fixed to the graphemes, as they are to the morphemes in language.

A commutation test can furnish the proof. The trunk of a human figure can be found portrayed in children's drawings by a round (RC), a triangle (TACJ), and a quadrangle (TCJ). A triangle may be used indiscriminately as the roof of a house, the sail of a boat, or the top of a pine tree. It may not be substituted, however, for the wheels of a cart, which must always be represented as round. Graphemes, therefore, in contrast to phonemes, seem to have an ambiguous status, being minimal differentiating units in a grapheme system and becoming morphemes in a context with other graphemes.

This double function suggests that graphemes could be iconic (or ''motivated'' in Saussurean terms), that is, structurally ''similar'' to (parts of) the objects they are used to represent. While Olivier (1974) does not wholly exclude a limited iconic grapheme function, he nevertheless insists that they are selectively acquired in the course of spontaneous exercises based on motoric and perceptual development. Only subsequently are they used to compose meaningful units stemming from the environment of the children. Since the environmental units are separate from the organism and permeated by culture, they must have existed prior to, and independently of, the children's ability to portray them, like words antedating the ability to speak them.

In support of the position that like letters, graphemes have no direct (motivated) connection to the content they portray, Olivier (1974) points out that the graphemes become more and more "regular" (e.g., symmetrical) as motor and perceptual coordination advances, hence following an independent rule of ontogenetic development.

Meaningfulness of Children's Drawings

A classification scheme will take a further look at how form is connected to meaning in children's drawings. Drawings from different age groups may be distributed by judges into three classes:

- Not meaningful drawings
- Partially meaningful drawings
- Completely meaningful drawings

When a set of children's drawings was so classified in a sorting study, the drawings in the first class contained only modulations or, at most, a few additional graphemes. According to Olivier, but in contradiction to Lurçat's observation, meaning is given to these drawings a posteriori by the children and may be changed in the course of time. Also, children are unable to repeat them. These drawings possess a global character, where the modulation refers to an object as a whole. The second class needs not to be considered here, because it just represents an intermediate stage. The third, which only contained drawings meaningful to the judges, featured graphemes that could be clearly attributed to Olivier's inventory. Children were able to reproduce them, and their meaning remained constant for their authors. According to Olivier, this meaning not only remains constant, but also antedates the drawings in that it may be "pronounced" prior to their composition. The drawings seem to be generated directly from the knowledge children have of the represented objects (intellectual realism; Luquet, 1927; Piaget & Inhelder, 1948/1967). This knowledge, which guides their hands, and the drawings, once complete, does not teach them anything they did not know before. It is in this sense that Olivier (1974) considers the graphemes of intellectual realism analogous to writing, since the signs in writing also only repeat on paper the words that the child already knows. It is only the combination of graphemes that, like the combination of letters, receives its meaning under the influence of the environment and culture in which the child grows up.

Paradoxically, according to Olivier (1974), it is not the graphemes, but the modulations replaced by the graphemes that are the earliest root of adult graphic creativity, since these are spontaneous motoric manifestations uninhibited by perceptual control.

With an investigation into the development of graphemes, the building blocks of children's drawings, I have concluded the survey of concepts and ideas devoted to the study of children's drawings in general.

The result is that the possibility of expressing mental images is clearly constrained by the maturation of perceptual-motor control at the efferent production end. At the same time it should be remembered that the images, too, undergo a gradual buildup. It is possible that the maturation of the perceptual motor apparatus and the buildup of images have a mutual influence.

PART II

Children's Drawings of Buildings

CHAPTER *7*

Introduction to the Study of Children's Drawings of Buildings

Why Study Drawings of Buildings?

Before I come to the central study of this book, I would like the sixth leg of the journey to focus attention on a very specific topic in the field of children's drawings. As I stated at the beginning of this book, the study of children's drawings amounts to an investigation of the mental image at its origin. And since there is no way of conducting experiments on children's imagination as a whole, we must confine the scope of the study to a particular topic. Why did I choose to study children's drawings of architecture? Aside from the fact that studies of the human figure have been exhaustive, and monographs on a chair (O'Shea, 1894) and on animals (Graewe, 1935) already exist, different building types recommend themselves for study because they are complex visual objects in children's environments. Their complexity even poses a problem for the imagination of grown-ups. This was shown, for example, in the drawings of graduate students who regularly underrated the number of windows of the college building that they entered daily (Norman & Rumelhart, 1975).

Because of their complexity, buildings are hard to describe verbally. This is reflected in architectural practice, which largely relies on drawings for conception and communication rather than on verbal reports. Certain building types, such as religious buildings, may even look different from one culture to the next, and they therefore constitute interesting drawing material for cross-cultural comparison. Moreover, children's drawings of buildings make an interesting subject for study because they are not as stereotyped as, for example, their drawings of

human beings, with ready-made images that only have to be copied (cf. Wilson
& Wilson, 1984). An exception is the ''little house''—one of the preferred
topics of children's drawings—which is often rendered stereotypically with a
pitched roof. But on the whole, complexity, iconicity, and cultural specificity
make buildings a suitable topic for a cross-cultural investigation of children's
iconic coding of their environment. In addition, I have already made a study of
adult recognition of different building functions (Krampen, 1979), and a comparison between these data and those from children's drawings promises interesting perspectives for further research.

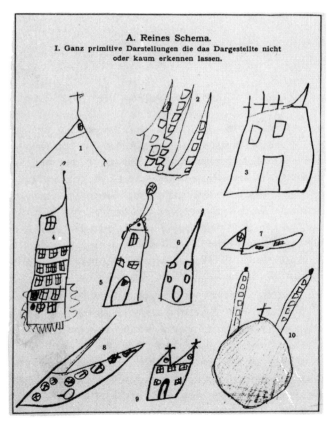

Figure 7.1. The development of church drawings according to Kerschensteiner (1905, pp. 278, 282,
292). 7.1a. "Pure schema. Highly primitive representation permitting little or no recognition of the
representation."

Figure 7.1b. "Pure schema. Representation of a church in form of a house."

Some Studies in the Literature

What do we already know from the literature on children's drawings of buildings? In an early survey, Kerschensteiner (1905, p. 219) found that houses represent one of the most frequent subjects of children's drawings, second only to humans and animals. When Kerschensteiner gave elementary school children the task of drawing a church, he found that 6-year-old children still could not (or could only vaguely) differentiate between a church and a house, or a building in general. Even drawings of churches made by older children were influenced by the more generalized image of a building. Windows and doors were rendered as in drawings of apartment buildings, while a steeple was frequently omitted. On the other hand, the roof was occasionally pointed in a pronounced way, and a cross on the roof often served as the only distinctive feature. Sometimes a clock was also attached to the roof.

Older children rendered the concept of a church building more clearly. The side elevation included elongated windows with round or pointed arches. The steeple was clearly distinguished from the nave and crowned with a cross or a knob. Sometimes ''transparencies'' were drawn, featuring church bells, church-goers, pews, etc. Finally, all schematism was dropped, and churches were rendered according to models in picture books or in the child's neighborhood (cf. a-f in Figure 7.1).

Figure 7.1c. "Representation of the church in elevation. Mixture of the phenomenal with the schematic."

Figure 7.1d. ''Representation in elevation. Phenomenal without schematism.''

One of Kerschensteiner's most significant findings was that girls largely renounced any attempt to draw perspective, whereas some of the boys began drawing perspective at the age of 11. By the age of 14, 50% of the boys drew in perspective, half of the results being failures, half of them correct.

Levinstein (1905) studied drawings of houses done by 100 boys and 100 girls between the ages of 6 and 14 years (Figure 7.2).

He found that even at the age of 14 only 54% drew their houses with more than one side. Houses drawn by children under 9 years were badly proportioned. They were extremely high structures with a pointed roof and countless windows. From these drawings developed houses with a moderate number of windows, but the windows were often situated in the wrong position on the facade and were badly distributed. Chimneys were drawn perpendicular to the oblique line of the

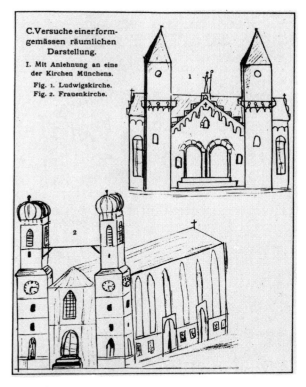

Figure 7.1e. "Attempt at a representation corresponding to form and space, with reference to Munich churches."

pointed roof. This phenomenon was also treated by Piaget and Inhelder (1948/1967), who considered it a failure of children up to the age of 7 to adopt a common horizon as a frame of reference for all elements of the drawing. Only at the ages of 10–12 years, according to Levinstein, did the houses begin to look "more decent." In a first stage of perspective, another side of the same house was simply added with its pointed roof, resulting in the impression of two houses or one house with two gables.

When children drew illustrations of stories, as did Levinstein's subjects on the German poem "Johnny-look-in-the-air," the number of houses included in the drawings rose steadily up to the age of 12 and then dropped drastically from 80% of the drawings to 56% at the age of 14. Levinstein asked some of the older children why they did not include houses in their drawings. They an-

Figure 7.1f. "Attempt at a spatial representation without reference to a Munich church"

swered, "I can't draw one," probably referring to their difficulty in coping with perspective.

A similar tendency toward regression at the age of 12 was found in a study on children's drawings of houses by Kerr (1937). She wanted to use house drawings as an indicator of the mental age of children, as had been done before with drawings of human figures. For this purpose she obtained house drawings from 555 normal, 70 mentally disturbed, and 60 emotionally disturbed children, all three groups covering the ages of 6 to 14 years.

Kerr found that the tendency toward elaboration increased with age. The percentages of curtains, two-sided houses, perspective, and door fittings rose steadily. The regression at the age of 12 could be seen by a drop in the frequency of doors, door fittings, tiles, two-sided houses, chimneys, steps, curtains, smoke, and houses in which only the upper windows were shown in the facade (see Figure 7.3).

Mentally defective children produced drawings comparable to those of normal children several years their juniors. Children diagnosed as neurotics drew a significantly larger number of long and thin houses than normal children.

Kerr concluded that children's drawings of houses are influenced by general

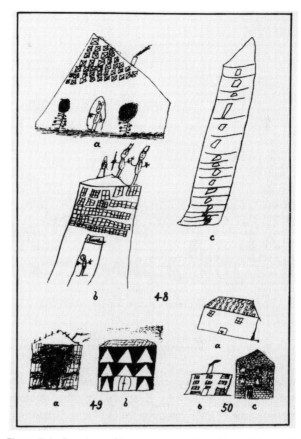

Figure 7.2. Drawings of houses from a study of Levinstein, 1905.

intellectual development (i.e., age) and emotional development or fixation. The use of house drawings for the diagnosis of mental development has been followed up in the House–Tree–Person Test (HTP) by Hammer (1964), later supplemented by Buck (1974).

Since only few statistical studies had been made with the HTP to test children's intelligence, and drawings of houses only had never been used for this purpose, Markham (1954) undertook such a study with samples of children aged 5–9 years. Along with the house drawings, she also obtained their IQ measures. She found that the house drawings of the 5-year-olds differed fundamentally from those of the older children.

Figure 7.2. (cont.)

In the older group the following items were incorporated in more than 50% of the drawings:

- Two-dimensional roof
- Chimney
- Two walls
- Door
- Door knob
- Windows in correct alignment
- Window panes

Only three items were significantly related to intelligence: the two-dimensional roof, two walls, and well-aligned windows. Items related to develop-mental levels were: two walls, well-aligned windows, correct placement of the house in the drawing space, window in the attic, a two-dimensional roof, and window shades or curtains. Markham (1954) concluded that drawings of houses are only useful for ''making a gross distinction between dull and superior children'' (p. 187).

In a further study on the subject, Kalyan-Masih (1976) had children draw a tree behind a house. She hypothesized that the front/behind conflict might be

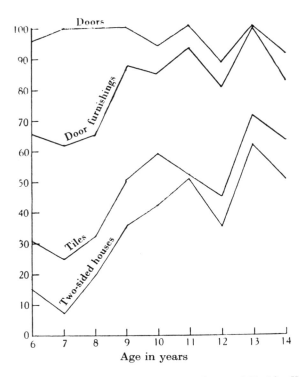

Figure 7.3. Regression in drawing development at the age of 12. After Kerr, 1937.

useful for revealing the children's strategies for coping with this problem when they were not yet able to draw concealed objects. More generally, she hoped to confirm the Luquet-Piaget sequence in children's drawing development (scribbling, fortuitous, failed, intellectual, and visual realism). Therefore, after completion of the drawing, she gave the children two intelligence tests and a selection of Piagetian tasks. She found that the Luquet-Piaget sequence could be inferred from the drawings. The drawing task also related significantly to the selected Piagetian measures. In addition, there seemed to be a synchronous development between the house-and-tree drawings and some cognitive measures in the two intelligence tests. Kalyan-Masih concluded that the house-and-tree drawings had a potential to assess the cognitive development of preschool children and, because of their independence of language, to be used in cross-cultural studies.

In another study, Ribault (1965) compared house drawings of children who grew up in a normal family (396 subjects) and children who were raised in an orphanage (141 subjects). The age range of the children was 4–12 years.

Each drawing was given a total score based on points given for the presence and kind of execution of specific details in the house drawing. A certain number of points were awarded for the size and position of the house on the drawing sheet, for transparencies, perspective, presence of roads, windows, doors, chimneys (with and without smoke), for drawings with two or more houses, with churches instead of houses, etc. The maximum score obtainable was 66 points. Among children growing up in families there were clear differences between age groups. Interestingly though, no differences were established between the drawings of boys and girls. The scores of orphans were clearly lower than the scores of children growing up in families (see Table 7.1).

In a study in a more phenomenological vein, the architect Rand (1972) muses about children's images of houses. At first he describes the steps by which the house becomes progressively more and more of a "symbol" for a child: The 5- or 6-year-old child experiences the home only with very elementary sociospatial distinctions. By 8 or 9 years of age, children begin to recognize general properties of the scenario played out by the family. By the age of 10 or 12, children have fully assimilated the rules guiding the sociospatial order of the home. According to Rand, these transformations in the child's experience are the result of the three phases in the development of representation postulated by Bruner (1966), those of enactive, iconic, and symbolic knowledge. The on-

Table 7.1. Comparison of Mean Scores on House Drawings by Children Raised at Home and in an Orphanage[a]

Age (yrs)	Upbringing	
	Home	Orphanage
4	11.77	—
5	16.62	—
6	19.52	19.50
7	24.03	21.00
8	27.06	22.70
9	29.27	27.55
10	31.31	30.29
11	34.38	32.52
12	36.10	33.00

[a]From Ribault, 1965.

togenesis of house drawings is embedded into this experiential process. For 6-year-old children, the concept of the house is an inextricable unity of form and expression. What the fixed features of a house are has still to be learned by them. The form may be modified to suit their own expression. The concept of construction has not yet developed to the point where a tall building is conceived of as a structure of steel and concrete. Hence the term *story* and words for related elements of construction (*beam, vault, pier,* etc.) still remain meaningless at this age. As the children begin to understand something about the means of construction, the placement of windows on the facade becomes more dependent on structure than on expression. Finally, children learn about the functionally determined aspects of buildings and start to vary them intentionally. It is at this point that the simple scheme of the house gives way to a more complex functional one. Along with an increasing knowledge about constructional means and functional aspects, the concept of *scale* develops. At the conclusion of this process, buildings of different sizes are drawn in their relative proportions. For Rand, the slow and ''conservative'' way in which children's drawings of houses change is a sign of the difficulty they have giving up old schemes of organization for new open-ended means. He sees the task of the architect as making evident the constructional and functional systems of building so that children can understand them more readily.

Children's Drawings of Different Building Types

The above studies of children's drawings of buildings were usually concerned with one building type only—in most cases the house. But in order to answer our question concerning the role of iconic representations in the interpretation of the built environment more than one building type must be studied. This is all the more necessary if we ask which system of distinctive architectural features is used by children to differentiate building types in their drawings.

Krampen *et al.* (1980) asked exactly this question. One hundred and two children aged 3–12 years from two nursery schools and two elementary schools in the Turkish town of Trabzon and from one elementary school in a nearby village were given the task of drawing six building types on one drawing sheet: office, factory, mosque, school, apartment building, and house.

The six drawings done by each child were scored on 26 variables. There were three groups of variables to be observed for each of the six building drawings. The first group of variables concerned drawing development in the sense of Luquet and Piaget (e.g., the occurrence of scribbles, transparencies, etc.). The second and largest group of variables observed in the drawings was building features (e.g., relative size of buildings, number of windows, occurrence of doors, etc.). The third group of variables consisted of additional drawing features (e.g., the occurrence of human figures, plants, etc.).

The reader should imagine that for each of the six building types, 26 observations were made, yielding ($6 \times 26 =$) 156 scores per child. With 102 children, a total of ($102 \times 156 =$) 15,912 measurements were obtained. In order to reduce this number of observations to a comprehensible size and to gain information on the variations and differences in the data, several analyses of variance were calculated.

At first, 12 of the drawing sheets with six drawings each were chosen at random and scored by four different persons independently to see how reliable the scoring system was. A special analysis of variance carried out on the ($4 \times 156 =$) 624 scores per child showed that not the raters but the building features provided the most significant source of variance in the data. This means that the four raters did not differ in their scoring but that the drawings differed in the building features used for the different building types. This was taken as an indication that children's drawings of buildings can be reliably scored.

In the main analysis of this study, the influence of the factors of age, building type, and sex on the variation in the data was investigated. The results showed that age, building type, and their interaction turned out to be significant sources of variance for many of the variables scored, whereas the sex of the children or any interaction of the other factors with sex did not appear to be responsible for variance in the data. This means that depending on age, the six building types were drawn differently by both girls and boys.

A special analysis of variance was made of two groups of 7-year-old elementary school children, one from the town and one from the nearby village. The sociogeographic origin of the children and its interaction with building type turned out to be significant sources of variance for some of the variables observed in the drawings. Interactions between age, sociogeographic origin, and building type were further demonstrated in a special comparison between the drawings of apartment buildings and houses made by all 102 children.

One informal impression from the data was that Luquet's and Piaget's phases of drawing development seemed to apply to Turkish children. This means that children from a culture very different from the one in which Luquet and Piaget made their original observations (France, Switzerland) showed the same drawing development. The main result of this study found a significant difference between children from urban and from rural schools, the latter lagging behind the former in drawing development for lack of visual access to some of the building types (e.g., office, factory, apartment building).

A second study (Krampen, 1986b) looked at cultural differences in the development of distinctive architectural features in children's drawings. The study was confined, however, to a comparison of two building types only— house and apartment building. The main hypothesis of this study was that there would be significant differences in the amount and kinds of distinctive features present in the drawings of houses and apartment buildings. These differences would occur at different age levels, but not in children at the same age level from different cultures. Furthermore, some differences between rural and urban children of the same age were expected. Drawings of a house and of an apartment building done by 95 Turkish children (same drawings as used in the Krampen *et al.,* 1980, study) and 97 German children from the Federal Republic of Germany were studied. The age of these children ranged from 3 to 12 years. Of the Turkish children, 35 attended nursery schools, 46 were in the first grade of elementary schools in the town of Trabzon, and 14 were in the first grade of an elementary school in a nearby village. Of the German children, 16 attended a nursery school in Schwäbisch Gmünd, southern Germany—a town similar in size to Trabzon— 40 were in the first grade of the elementary school of that town, and 41 were in the first grade of an elementary school in a village nearby. The pairs of drawings (house and apartment building) from each child were scored for their relationship on five variables: size of building shape, number of stories, number of windows, verticality of shape, and type of roof. To see whether or not the differences in these variables were purely chance, binomial and chi-square tests were carried out on the data under the hypothesis that the house would be smaller in shape; would have less stories, less windows, and less verticality than the apartment building; and would also feature a pointed roof, as opposed to the flat roof of the apartment building. Subsequently, various groups from both the same and different age levels were tested for homogeneity with respect to the five variables and pooled if no significant differences could be found. The results in Table 7.2 show that to a significant degree older children in both cultures used the five scoring variables in the predicted way, but that there were significant differences between older and younger children.

Also, significant differences were found between rural and urban children in the use of the variables size of shape and form of roof. No striking differences could be detected, however, between the drawings of Turkish and German children of the same age and sociogeographic origin (i.e., village or town).

In summary, there appeared to be no difference between the children from

Table 7.2. Age Differences in the Use of Five Scoring Variables in Drawings of Apartment Buildings and Houses by Turkish and German Children

| | Use of five variables | | | |
| | Turkish children | | German children | |
Variable	Nursery age 3/4 vs. 5/6	Nursery vs. elementary	Nursery age 3/4 vs. 5	Nursery vs. elementary
Size	H < A:p < .01	H < A:p < .001	n.s.	n.s.
Stories	H < A:p < .05	H < A:p < .001	n.s.	n.s.
Windows	H < A:p < .02	H < A:p < .001	n.s.	H < A:p < .01
Verticality	H < A:p < .001	H < A:p < .001	n.s.	H < A:p < .02
Flat roof	n.s.	H < A:p < .01	n.s.	n.s.

Note: H, house; A, apartment building; n.s., nonsignificant; p, probability.

two rather different cultures—Turkish and German—in the variables measured in their drawings. In both cultures, town children distinguished more clearly between apartment buildings and houses than did village children, presumably because children in towns have had more visual exposure to apartment buildings than children in villages.

   In a third study (Brucker, 1982), part of the data from the German children in the investigation just described was compared with drawings done by physically handicapped German children, most of them suffering from cerebral palsy. The hypothesis was that bodily impaired children would lag behind their nonhandicapped peers in the general ability to draw (as measured by a "global rating") and in the special ability to differentiate in their drawings between the six building types (office, factory, church, school, apartment building, and house). The sample of handicapped children consisted of 28 girls and boys aged 6–7 years and 39 girls and boys aged 8–12 years, all attending a school for the physically handicapped in Ulm (southern Germany). Their drawings were compared with those of 31 peers aged 6–7 and 16 peers aged 8–12 from the German elementary school children in the Krampen (1986b) study. The technique of "global rating" will be described in more detail in the methods section of this book (Chapter 8). For the purpose of reporting on the Brucker (1982) study, it is sufficient to note that it consisted of a five-point scale. Criteria of the scale were based on the drawing properties in the various stages of development established by Luquet (1927) and Piaget and Inhelder (1948/1967).

   The variables considered to be important in the framework of this comparison between nonhandicapped and handicapped children were the global rating score, the age, and the group (i.e., handicapped vs. nonhandicapped). The influence of these factors and of their interaction was analyzed by the technique of loglinear models that will be described in detail in the methods section (Chapter 8). In summary, this technique can be used to test whether one or more of these variables was responsible for the frequency distribution of the rating scores obtained, and which of these variables could be eliminated from the model describing the effects. The frequency distribution of the global rating scores in the Brucker study is given in Table 7.3.

Table 7.3 shows that in both age groups, nonhandicapped children tend to have higher scores than handicapped children. The statistical significance of the source variables and of their interaction is given in Table 7.4.

Table 7.4 shows that the variable "global rating" and its interaction with age and with group, and the interaction between age and group are highly significant. This means that the global rating (i.e., stage of drawing development) has the largest effect in this comparison. This effect interacts, on the one hand, with age: for both groups it is true that the older the children are, the higher their scores tend to be. On the other hand, there is a highly significant interaction between the global rating and group: children in the nonhandicapped group have higher scores than their handicapped counterparts. In order to reduce all drawings to a common denominator, Brucker (1982) constructed "phantom drawings" from the measures of central tendency for size of building shape, verticality, form of the roof, presence of a secondary building, number of stories, number of windows, size and verticality of windows. The method by which phantom drawings are constructed will be dealt with in the methods section of this book (Chapter 8). At this point it is sufficient to understand that the phantom drawings are composed from all the drawings investigated, just as criminal investigators compose the drawings of wanted persons from many different

Table 7.3. Frequency Distribution of Global Rating Scores[a]

	Frequencies			
	Handicapped children		Nonhandicapped children	
Global rating score	6–7 yrs	8–12 yrs	6–7 yrs	8–12 yrs
1	1	0	0	0
2	2	0	1	0
3	14	20	1	0
4	3	19	21	5
5	0	0	8	11

[a]From Brucker, 1982.

Table 7.4. Global Rating, Age, Physical Impairment
and Their Interactions[a]

Effects and interactions	df	Chi-square	p
Age (A)	1	0.15	.6976
Global rating score (R)	4	91.51	.0000
Group[b] (G)	1	1.36	.2433
AR	4	20.75	.0004
AG	1	25.17	.0000
RG	4	80.63	.0000
ARG	4	0.12	.9982

[a]From Brucker, 1982.
[b]Handicapped vs. nonhandicapped children.

testimonies. The phantom drawings for the handicapped children are given separately for the 6–7 year age range and the 8–12 year age range in Figures 7.4 and 7.5.

In order to pinpoint the variables that discriminated between the drawings of physically handicapped and nonhandicapped children, a discriminant analysis

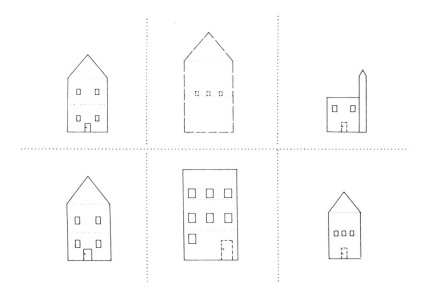

Figure 7.4. Phantom drawings of six building types (top left to bottom right: office, factory, church, school, apartment building, house) resulting from the analysis of drawings made by physically handicapped children 6–7 years of age.

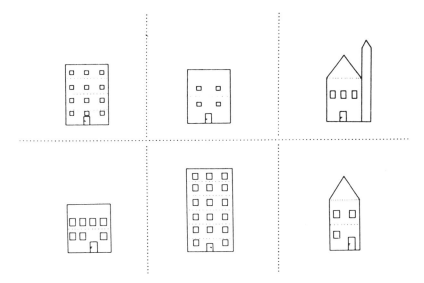

Figure 7.5. Phantom drawings of six building types (top left to bottom right: office, factory, church, school, apartment building, house) resulting from the analysis of drawings made by physically handicapped children 8–12 years of age.

was carried out over a large number of variables. Brucker (1982) found that the following 10 variables distinguished the drawings of the handicapped children from those of the nonhandicapped children:

- Handicapped children drew more rounded roofs.
- They drew fewer stories in the apartment buildings.
- The windows in their apartment buildings were more vertical.
- They had fewer smokestacks in their drawings of factories.
- They drew fewer shed roofs on their factories.
- They drew fewer saddle roofs in perspective.
- Their house shapes were more vertical.

On the whole, Brucker's data supported her hypothesis that handicapped children would lag behind their nonhandicapped peers in general drawing development and specifically in the ability to differentiate the six building types in their drawings. She explained this lag by the difference in quantity and quality of access to the environment: handicapped children have restricted access to the environment because of their bodily impairment and also because they are overprotected by adults. This lack of experience delays the development of internal models of objects present in the environment and hence the ability to render them in drawings.

The Influence of Physical or Mental Impairment on the Development of Drawing Ability

Brucker's study questions the influence of physical impairment on the development of drawing ability. An answer to this question should help clarify whether drawing development is a natural or cultural matter. If impairment delays development, only physical factors are involved.

There is some evidence in the literature that the retarded drawing ability of children with cerebral palsy might be due to their disturbed body image. In particular, their drawings of the human figure have been interpreted as projections of their own distorted body image. The concept of body image goes back to Schilder (1935), who held that "the way children draw human figures really reflects their knowledge and sensory experience of the body image" (p. 106). The problem of personality projection in the drawing of the human figure was emphasized by Machover (1949, 1953). In fact, Wysocky and Whitney (1965) found differences between crippled and noncrippled children in Machover's Draw-a-Person test. Wysocki and Wysocki (1973) investigated drawings of the human figure for differences between normal and mentally retarded children. In comparison with the former, the drawings of the latter were larger in size, had less clothing, less detail, and exhibited less erasures. Interestingly, they were less symmetrical, and the figures showed a rigid horizontal positioning of the arms.

Tabary (1964) compared the ability of children to draw a man and to copy geometric figures. The result was that for feeble-minded, normally intelligent, and cerebral-palsied children, the development of the spatial aspect of the body image "was subject to general laws of representation applicable to any other object" (p. 643). In all three groups of children, the scores on human-figure drawings were the same as on geometric items. Tabary concluded that "from birth and throughout childhood there is a precise parallelism between the child's body scheme, as far as he can express it, and his capacity to express his geometrical understanding of the world around him" (p. 643). For the purposes of this book, this conclusion suggests that building drawings would be equally subject to a parallelism with the child's body scheme. A distorted body scheme would then be paralleled by distorted building drawings.

A similar parallelism was noted by Williams (1964). She found a significant correlation of confusion and distortion of the body image assessed from drawings with a child's distracted behavior, short attention span, and anxiety about separation from his or her mother.

The results of an investigation by Paine (1964) showed that some of the drawings of children with chronic brain syndromes resemble those of normal children at earlier stages of development, while others were qualitatively distorted and often bizarre.

Other investigators who tried a similar approach found no support in their data for the projection hypothesis. Silverstein and Robinson (1956) obtained three sets of human-figure drawings (self, same sex, and opposite sex) from 22 children in a chronic state of poliomyelitis. On inspection they found that more than three-quarters of these children seemed to represent their disability directly or indirectly in their drawings. A comparison with a normal control group matched for age, sex, and IQ, however, revealed significant differences between the two groups in only 10 out of 55 scoring items. Furthermore, judges experienced in the psychodiagnostic use of figure drawings could not differentiate between the drawings of the disabled and normal children at more than a normal level of chance.

Other evidence against the assumption that projection of a distorted body image influences children's drawings comes from Centers and Centers (1963). They wanted to test the following two hypotheses:

1. A Draw-a-Person test assumed to represent a body image will distinguish between the drawings of amputee and nonamputee children.
2. Amputee children will have more conflict and defensiveness about their bodies than will nonamputee children. This will come out in their drawings of themselves.

Twenty-six children between the ages of 5 and 12 years who had upper-extremity amputations were equated with the same number of nonhandicapped children for sex, chronological age, and mental age. Both groups were asked to draw a person of each sex and a picture of themselves. Only the self-portrait showed differences between the two groups—primarily in the treatment of the arms. No significant differences in the indicators of conflict and defensiveness (hypothesis 2) were found between the drawings of the two groups. Centers and Centers concluded that the amputee children represented their bodies realistically and did not project, on the whole, conflict and defensiveness in their drawings.

Abercrombie (1964) suggested that the contradiction between evidence for and against the projection hypothesis might be reduced if the following terminology proposed by Smythies (1953) was adopted:

- Body schema: a subconscious, purely physiological mechanism.
- Body image: a visual, mental, or memory image of the body.
- Body concept: a constellation of memories and beliefs concerning the physical body.
- Perceived body: the body as it is currently perceived.

Abercrombie (1964) argued that in children with cerebral palsy the *body schema* must be in disorder because of a continuous abnormal sensory input from disordered movement. Children with somatic sensory impairment might well have *perceived body* disorders. The *body image* and *body concept* of these children is difficult to investigate. But when children indicate their handicap in drawings of themselves, they do not project a disorder of body image or body concept; instead, they realistically show that they know what their body is like (cf. Centers & Centers, 1963).

To prove this point, Abercrombie and Tyson (1966) gave a group of 24 children with cerebral palsy and 23 nonhandicapped 6-year-olds the Goodenough Draw-a-Man Test and had them copy 10 simple geometric figures. A "Goodenough mental age" was estimated from the human figures, and a "copying mental age" was estimated from the copies for the cerebral-palsied children. The estimates of the mental ages from Goodenough's test were similar to those from the copies. This result led Abercrombie and Tyson to conclude that the Draw-a-Man Test did not measure body-image disorder but a general difficulty in drawing, as also manifested by the copies.

Moreover, the human-figure drawings of the normal children often showed peculiarities that could have been interpreted as indicators of physical impairment. It cannot be concluded, therefore, that children with cerebral palsy represent physical impairment in their drawings until it is proven that they show these indicators more frequently than do nonhandicapped children of the same Goodenough mental age.

This extensive discussion of evidence for and against the influence of the body image in children's drawings, especially on those of human figures, was necessary to add to the discussion of the results of Brucker's (1982) study. Brucker's cerebral-palsied children are not only retarded in their drawing development because they have been less exposed to the environment than the normally developing child. They are also retarded because of "general difficulties in drawing" (Abercrombie, 1964). But of what does this general difficulty in drawing consist? I will later show evidence indicating that this difficulty might arise from difficulties in the acquisition of symmetric graphemes.

Cultural Comparison—A Qualitative Pilot Study

General Remarks

We are now approaching the goal of our journey: the study of different building types in the drawings of children of different ages and from different cultures. The following pages should prepare us for the last leg of the journey. They consist of juxtaposed pairs of building drawings that were partly used in the central study of this book. Each pair consists of one drawing by a Turkish child and one by a German child. The children are matched for age, so we can concentrate on possible cultural differences with the developmental variable age remaining constant. The drawings are divided into three groups, following the stages of drawing development as formulated by Luquet (1927) and Piaget and Inhelder (1948/1967).

The First Stage: Fortuitous and Failed Realism (Synthetic Incapacity)

The first set of drawings documents the developmental transition of children from the stage of sensorimotor intelligence to the preoperatory phase (Figures 7.6–7.17).

As pointed out earlier, the stage of sensorimotor intelligence serves to develop the coordination of children's perceptions and their motor activity. Note that once this stage has been completed in the first drawings, the first attempts to form shapes out of pure scribbles appear. At first, only closed and round shapes are opposed to open and linear ones. These serve as multipurpose symbols representing many things. The same shapes can represent different buildings at different times. Soon, round, closed shapes are opposed to angular, closed shapes. The relationships of including shapes within a larger shape, placing one shape next to another, or one on the borderline of another are also used purposefully by the child. Many children drew only a few of the six building types (office, factory, mosque or church, school, apartment building, house) that they had been asked to produce. Some did not even try to draw more than two or three.

Figure 7.6a. Melda was a 3½-year-old girl in the city nursery school of Trabzon. When she was asked to draw a house (after she had already completed an office and a factory), she reverted to pure scribbling. She obviously liked the traces her rhythmic movement left on the paper.

Figure 7.6b. Martin, a 3-year-old boy in the city nursery school of Schwäbisch Gmünd, was the youngest child in the German nursery school group. In the space on the drawing sheet reserved for the apartment building he scribbled with the blunt end of his pencil because he had found out that this was also a way of leaving traces of paper.

Figure 7.7a. When Melda was first asked to draw an office building, she formed two closed shapes out of rhythmic scribbles. The round marks on the borderline of the round shape were used to express that there was something attached to the borderline, perhaps a corner. A scribble was placed within the round shape. The elongated shape was situated outside the round form. Thus, closed forms, inside, on the border, and outside were the four basic notions Melda used in this drawing.

Figure 7.7b. For the office building, Martin drew an open form surrounding another open form. He added a lot of scribbles made with both the pointed and the blunt ends of his pencil.

Figure 7.8a. When asked to draw a factory, Melda, starting with pure scribbles, completed a closed form. This form surrounded the scribbles. Melda did not try to draw a mosque, a school, or an apartment building.

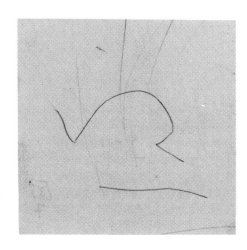

Figure 7.8b. When asked to draw a school, Martin managed to repeat an open form similar to that of his office building and to draw a heavy line.

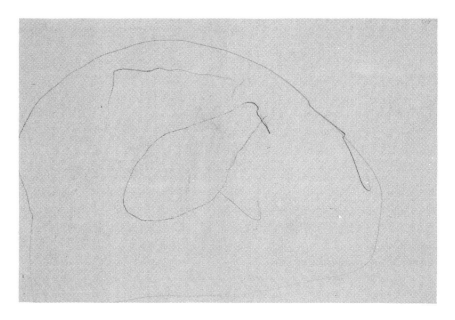

Figure 7.9a. Rahsan was a girl of 3½ years in the city nursery school of Trabzon. She drew a house by enclosing one round shape within another made with a large motor gesture.

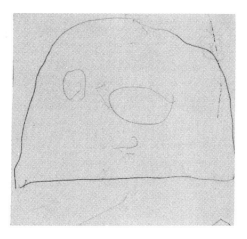

Figure 7.9b. Daniela was a 3-year-old girl in the city nursery school of Schwäbisch Gmünd. For a school she drew a nice closed form consisting of two segment meeting each other. Two other round forms are enclosed within this. The resulting similarity to the drawing of her Turkish peer Rahsan (see Figure 7.9a) is amazing.

Figure 7.10a. Rahsan's office building is a rectangular, closed shape enclosing a round shape and some scribbles. Thus she tried to oppose angular closed shapes to round closed shapes. Because she still found it very hard to draw the straight lines of a rectangle, she used the border of the paper for orientation. Rahsan did not draw the mosque, the school, or the apartment building.

Figure 7.10b. Daniela almost succeeded in drawing a rectangle for a factory.

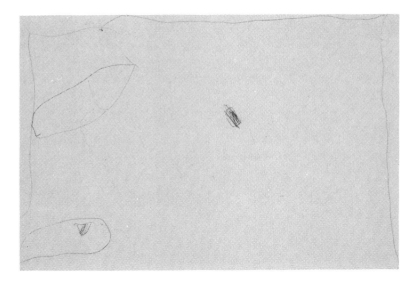

Figure 7.11a. Rahsan's drawing of the factory also uses an angular enclosing shape. At the bottom she saved drawing the line by using the border of the paper instead. She enclosed round shapes and some scribbles. Rahsan made the office and the factory angular and the house round.

Figure 7.11b. When Daniela was asked to draw a house, she reverted to scribbling after having attempted a straight line. Some of the scribbles are oriented toward the horizontal and vertical frame of the drawing sheet.

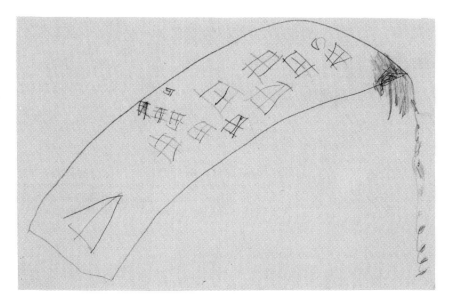

Figure 7.12a. Iraz, a 4-year-old boy in the city nursery school of Trabzon, drew his house as a closed form composed of curved lines converging in one point: the roof. The house shape includes many windows and a triangular door, divided in the middle. From the top of the roof the smoke of the chimney emerges in the form of scribbles and loops. Iraz had not yet learned that the bottom of the page is a convention for "ground" and the top for "sky." He drew his house diagonally across the page to make it as tall as possible.

Figure 7.12b. Holger was a 3-year-old boy in the city nursery school of Schwäbisch Gmünd. He drew the apartment building as a triangle enclosing angular forms that represented a door (with a handle) and windows. The chimney is typically oriented to the left of the triangle and not to the horizontal base of the sheet. The house (not shown here) was almost identical to the apartment building, but much smaller.

Figure 7.13a. For the factory, Holger placed an open rectangular form in such a way that it was closed by the bottom of the drawing sheet. In the rectangle he included a door (with handle) and three windows with curtains (or shutters).

The Second Stage: Intellectual Realism

The second set of drawings (Figures 7.18–7.29) shows the work of elementary school children in the preoperatory phase. Consequently, scribbling has now been abandoned. Building shapes are rendered by rectangles and squares, excepting the mosque, which is given a dome, and all include windows. However, at the early stages of this development there are still some blanks on the drawing sheets where the child seemed to have no mental image of the building type. Also, the rectangular forms with windows are not detailed enough to distinguish the different building functions; rather, they serve as multipurpose forms. The drawings at this stage of development culminate in intellectual realism with its "transparencies," that is, drawings of buildings showing what exists inside them. Sometimes, the inside is even preferred to symbolize the whole building, especially when there is no clear conception of what the building should look like from the outside. Thus, at this stage of development, we find a rich assortment of viewpoints and pseudo-perspectives.

The drawings were created at the schools attended by the Turkish and German girls and boys. The three Turkish subgroups contain drawings done by two children each, with each pair going to a different school. One school was located in a rural area (Cimenli), another in a city (Trabzon), and the third on a university campus (Karadeniz Technical University). For each school, examples of the beginning and peak of this stage of development are presented to show that both phases of intellectual development are present in all three schools. The German children visited two elementary schools—a village school in Bartholomae, near Schwäbisch Gmünd, and a city school in Schwäbisch Gmünd.

Figure 7.13b. When Iraz drew an office building, he used (like Rahsan, see Figure 7.10a) the borderline of the page for orientation to draw a large rectangle. But he did not yet accept the convention that the borders of the sheet might represent the ground and sky. Therefore, he placed the triangular door on the right side of the paper. But his pseudo-writing along the other side of the building points in the opposite direction of the door. Included in the rectangle are windows and what appears to be people, together with a few scribbles. Iraz did not try to draw the mosque, the school, or the apartment building.

Figure 7.14a. Iraz drew the factory as a square including windows and scribbles. From this square, open forms emerged, indicating perhaps television antennas and what seems to be a flag. He kept refusing to use the borderline of the paper as orientation for what is up and what is down.

Figure 7.14b. For Holger, the school is a rectangle similar to that of the factory, but smaller. Smoke issues from the roof.

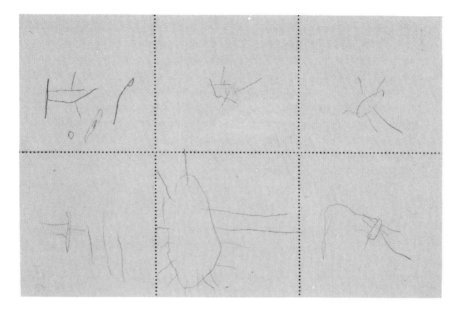

Figure 7.15a. Adlin was a 3-year-old girl in the university nursery school of Trabzon. Adlin drew all six buildings. From left to right, you find in the first row: office, factory, mosque; in the second row: school, apartment building, and house. She mostly used closed, round shapes, adding linear marks in a circular fashion. Some of the shapes are more angular, and there are some open forms such as lines running parallel. She varied the sizes of the multipurpose shapes to indicate differences (e.g., big apartment building, little house). The linear marks radiating from the round shapes like rays from the sun are a preferred motive of children at this stage of development. These marks indicate modifications to the closed shapes (corners, protrusions, etc.).

Children of the same age, similar stage of development, and similar school type in Turkey and in Germany are placed side by side for comparison, so you can get a feeling of what the central study of this book will be about.

The Third Stage: Visual Realism

The last set of pictures (Figures 7.30–7.34) is the work of elementary school children from the city school of Trabzon, from the school on the university campus, from the city school of Schwäbisch Gmünd, and from the village school of Bartholomae. It shows the transition in drawing development taking place between the preoperatory stage and the stage of concrete mental operations

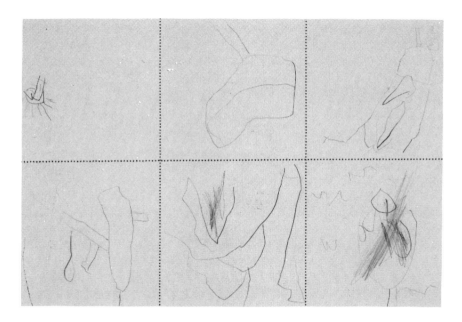

Figure 7.15b. Thomas, a 3½-year-old boy in the city nursery school of Schwäbisch Gmünd, drew (above, left) a round form including other round forms and a scribble for the office. For the factory (above, center) he tried to obtain closed forms by a series of open curves attached to each other. The school (below, left) was drawn by turning the paper in another direction. The chimney on the roof points downward, as does the chimney on the apartment building (below, center). The house (below, right) is a combination of round, open, and closed forms and scribbles.

manifested by visual realism. At the ages of about 13 to 14 years, this stage is followed by the accomplishment of formal operations. Many concepts in drawing that guarantee visual realism are acquired fairly late in the stage of concrete operations. Perspective, sections, rotation and the unfolding of solids, proportion, and the overall coordination of perspective and proportion presuppose very difficult mental operations and are acquired only at the age of 10 or later. This set of drawings illustrates this development with examples by boys and girls aged 7,

---
→

Figure 7.16b. Regina, a girl of 4 in the city nursery school of Schwäbisch Gmünd, tried to draw a series of rectangles. The office (above, left) is a square and has two windows and a chimney. In the factory drawing (above, center) she failed to draw the square and closed the form with a curve. The church (above, right) consists of a series of open interlocking forms closed by the lower part of the frame—an attempt to draw a complex form, perhaps a tower. The school (below, left) features a roof (?) and a scribble. The apartment building (below, center) has a roof with an allusion to a pointed gable. She started to draw a house but then gave up.

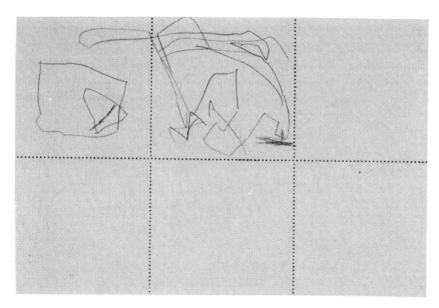

Figure 7.16a. Beyza was a 3½-year-old girl in the university nursery school of Trabzon. With her large motoric gestures, she succeeded in forming the office (above left) as a square including a triangle (a door?). The factory (above, center) is a jumble of round and angular lines that form some superimposed closed shapes. She tried to draw the school (below, left) by making three separate, round, closed forms. But that did not satisfy her and she erased them. She did not try the mosque, the apartment building, or the house.

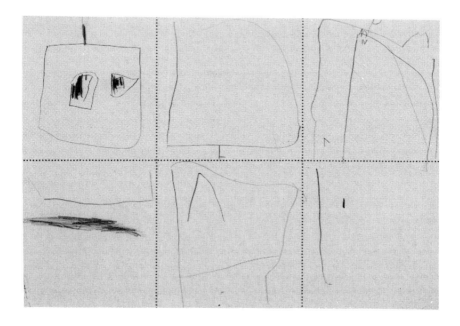

Figure 7.17a. Erdogan was a 3½-year-old boy in the university nursery school of Trabzon. Erdogan drew a rectangle for the office (above, left) and included windows. A jumble of loose scribbles emerges from the rectangle. The factory (above, center) was depicted as a closed form featuring a round part, two corners, and a closed, round shape. The external shape is marked by radiating lines. The mosque (above, right) is a large, round shape marked by "sunrays." The school (below, left) was formed with five, closed and angular shapes, one of which is a rectangle containing two little people. The apartment building (below, center) is a square including windows. The house (below, right) is a beautiful egg shape with two protrusions; a small mark was included. Erdogan also did not use the coordinate system of the paper as a convention for "up" and "down" (see the people in the school and the smoke emerging from the apartment building).

9, and 12. There is a progressive abandoning of pseudo-perspective in favor of linear perspective and an increasing sense of proportion. Note, however, that in the development toward visual realism a loss of the sense of richness appears to take place, which was conveyed by the naive "medley of viewpoints" prevailing during the phase of intellectual realism.

→

Figure 7.18a. Zeynep was a 7-year-old girl in the village school of Cimenli. She drew the house (above, left), the apartment building (above, center), and the school (above, right), but none of the other buildings. Her house and school are squares subdivided by horizontal and vertical lines into four compartments each. The house features windows with what appears to be curtains. The school is differentiated from the house by its size and by the obligatory Turkish flag next to it. Zeynep wanted to start the drawing of the apartment building but didn't have a precise idea of what an apartment building actually is. So she left the drawing unfinished.

Figure 7.17b. Fiola, a 3-year-old girl in the city nursery school of Schwäbisch Gmünd, populated her buildings with tadpole men. The office (above, left) has a complex form that in turn included other open and closed forms. The factory (above, center) is a nice rectangle with two smoking chimneys (Fiola drew this building upside down). For the church (above, right) she did not succeed in closing the forms. The school (below, left) and apartment building (below, center) are closed, angular forms enclosing other forms. The house (below, right) in contrast, is round and contains a large tadpole man. Fiola commented: "They often say that only mama lives in the house, because papa is working."

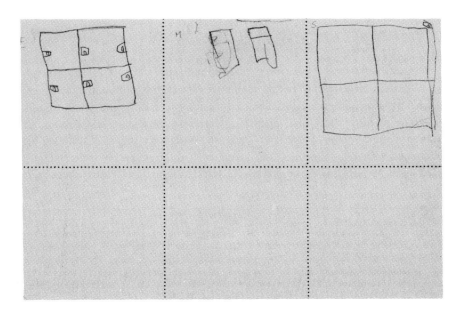

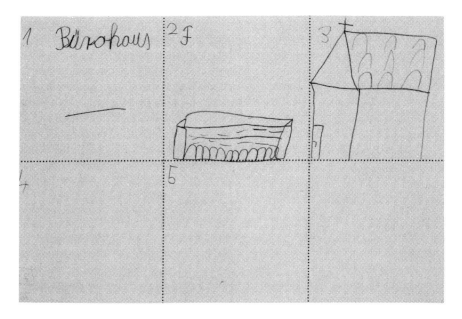

Figure 7.18b. Silke, a 7-year-old girl attending the village school of Bartholomae, was able to write the German word for "office building" (above, left), but she had no internalized image of it. The factory (above, center) was drawn in pseudo-perspective with many gates. In the church (above, right), the steeple and nave, with tiled roof, were probably contracted into one pseudo-perspective. On top of the steeple there is a cross. The school, the apartment building, and the house were not drawn.

Conclusions

What can be learned from this qualitative observation of building drawings? At what age do children acquire the distinction between different types of buildings? The pictures show that regardless of their environment and culture, all children—some sooner, some later—pass the obligatory stages of drawing development: failed, intellectual, and visual realism. But the environment may speed up or hamper this development. A child living in a rural area where there

---→

Figure 7.19b. Anna was a 7-year-old girl in the village school of Bartholomae. Anna's office building was drawn in pseudo-perspective. She also showed, by transparency, two people sitting inside at opposite ends of a table (perhaps a clerk and a client?). The factory (above, center) is furnished with many arched windows, two smokestacks, and a hoisting crane. The church (above, right) is a building with many arched windows and a cross on the roof. The school (below, left) was drawn in the same pattern as the church, but the windows are rectangular and larger. The apartment building is represented with seven stories and a flat roof. The house has three stories and a gabled roof.

Figure 7.19a. Zeliha, a 7-year-old girl in the village school of Cimenli drew the house (above, left), with curtained windows, in pseudo-perspective. It is in proportion to the three-story apartment building (above, center) and the school (above, right). The school, likewise in pseudo-perspective, is distinguished by the Turkish flag. The mosque (below, left), drawn on a different scale to the house, the apartment building, and the school, features a minaret and stairs. The factory (below, center), drawn on the same scale as the mosque, features a chimney. The office (below, right) is rendered from the inside of the building, with desk and office chair, a seat, and what appears to be a stove.

Figure 7.20a. Mine, a 7-year-old girl in the city school of Trabzon, symbolizes the office (above, left) by what could be a chair. Her factory (above, center) has five stories. The mosque (above, right), rendered very small in comparison with the apartment building, has a minaret and a dome. Next to it stands a girl (Mine?). The school (below, left) again distinguished by a flag, has three stories. The apartment building (below, center) has four stories, a flat roof, and two television antennas. The house (below, right) has two stories and a smoking chimney on the roof. Mine used nonarchitectural features (a girl, a flag, television antennas, and smoke) and the form of the roof to distinguish the buildings.

are no office buildings or factories will probably develop an image of these buildings later than a city child exposed to them frequently.

The drawings suggest that some distinctive architectural features of buildings are learned between the ages of 4 and 7 years (the peaked roof of the individual house, dome and minaret of the mosque). Other buildings are distinguished by nonarchitectural features: the school is already identified by the flag at preschool age by some Turkish children. The concept of an apartment building, and especially that of an office building, is probably acquired later, the apartment building being distinguished from the house by size and number of stories as was shown in a previous quantitative study (Krampen, 1986b). There remains a good deal of confusion between the apartment and office buildings, probably because they are in fact difficult to distinguish. This is the case at least

Figure 7.20b. Eva Maria was a 7-year-old girl in the school in Schwäbisch Gmünd. Eva Maria's office building (above, left) is a four-story building with a pointed, tiled roof. There are curtains at the windows. Through one of the windows one spots a little man sitting in front of a typewriter. The building had many letter boxes and four door plates with bell buttons. The factory (above, center) is marked by a closed gate and a thick smokestack. The church (above, right) features a main steeple with a clock and decorated portal. In addition, there are two small turrets on the roof, one with a church bell, the other with a second clock. The school (below, left) is a multistory building with a gabled roof. The windows are exact squares that Eva Maria drew by using a stencil. In comparison, the apartment building (below, center) has fewer stories, larger windows without curtains and a flat roof. The house (below, right) has two stories, a gabled roof, and curtains in the windows.

in the city of Trabzon, where many "modern" multistory buildings serve both functions.

On the other hand, there are many private homes in smaller German towns that are used additionally as offices. Hence, it is no surprise that these two building types are confused by the younger children, or, for that matter, by anyone.

The drawing sample shows no particular difference in the development of girls and boys. Also, there seems to be no noticeable difference in the drawing development of the Turkish and German children. Children from both cultures first seem to develop a common stock of graphemes, which they subsequently use to represent their mental images of objects that are present in their particular

Figure 7.21a. Nagahan was a 7-year-old boy in the city school of Trabzon. Nagahan used some detail inside the office (above, left), namely, a person standing at a desk with a typewriter. The factory (above, center) was rendered in transparency, showing many little rooms with people "working like ants." The factory has two smokestacks. The mosque (above, right) comprises a dome, a minaret, and four water faucets with seats in front of them for performing the Moslem washing ritual. A little man (Nagahan?) with his head covered and wearing a tie is standing next to the mosque. On the roof of the school (below, left) is a Turkish flag. Nagahan started to color the school brown (roof) and yellow (walls). The apartment building (below, center) has three or four stories. On the roof Nagahan drew what appears to be a row of balconies. In the drawing of the two-story house (below, right), stairs lead up to the door, the chimney is smoking, and the roof is drawn in pseudo-perspective.

cultural environment. Iconic problem solving in children seems to unfold ontogenetically in the same way as problem solving in the adult world. Architects, for example, often start with a general portrayal of topological relationships on a napkin and end up with metric, proportional, and perspectival precision. The parsimony in the application of graphic means (e.g., the use of multipurpose "stamps") and also the tendency to stick to past solutions are traits in problem solving common to both children and adults. Unfortunately, iconic problem solving seems to be given up by most children when letters and numbers become emphasized in school.

Figure 7.21b. Alexandra, a 7-year-old girl in the city school of Schwäbisch Gmünd, drew the office building (above, left) with a tiled, pointed roof and only two stories. Alexandra's factory (above, center), executed with a ruler, consists of a tower (or smokestack?) and a flat building. At the factory gate she placed five bell buttons. In her church (above, right), the steeple is connected with the high nave almost in one perspective. One of the arched windows contains a stained glass picture of a human figure. The school (below, left) is as in Eva Maria's drawing (see Figure 7.20b), a multistory building with a gabled roof. The building and windows were drawn with a ruler or a stencil, but the crossbars were entered freehand. The apartment building (below, center) is similar to the school but with fewer stories. The house (below, right) was drawn with one story and a picture window with curtains and a bunch of flowers.

A Glance Backward and Some Open Questions

At the beginning of this book, I announced a complicated journey from the general to the specific, from the periphery to the center of a series of concentric circles. We have almost reached the center, where lies the study that should clarify some of the points that have remained uncertain during the voyage. But before I begin to formulate the hypotheses of that study, let me just look back at some of the legs of this journey.

It started out with Piaget's general theory of mental development. Embed-

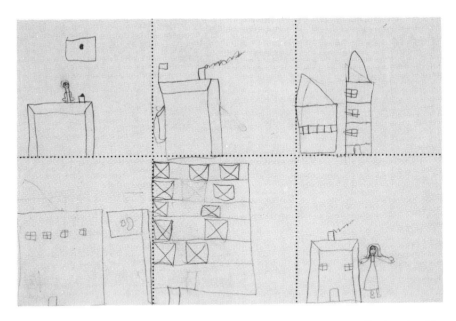

Figure 7.22a. Necla was a 6½-year-old girl in the university school of Trabzon. She drew the office (above, left) from inside, with a desk (in pseudo-perspective), a person sitting behind it, and the obligatory picture of Kemal Atatürk (rendered by a dot) above the desk. The factory (above, center), in pseudo-perspective, features some protruding tubes (spotted, perhaps, on the Trabzon cement factory), and a flag and a smokestack on the roof. Necla's mosque (above, right) is a building covered by a dome with a separate minaret. The school (below, left) is distinguished by a flag. The apartment building (below, center) has six stories and a flat roof. The two-story house (below, right) in pseudo-perspective (like the office desk!) features a smoking chimney. It is well related in size to the apartment building, but the lady standing next to it is almost as tall as the house.

ded in this theory is a phase, the emergence of imagination, in which the mental image appears and develops. The mental image was described by Piaget as an internalized imitation of perceptual activity that occurs while the object of perception is actually out of sight (Piaget & Inhelder, 1966/1969).

This construct was attacked by those who hold that the metaphor of an image or a picture is wrong because it presupposes some kind of mind's eye "seeing" an image (Pylyshyn, 1973). They proposed their own metaphor instead—the computer. According to this metaphor, our knowledge of the environment is stored as strings of propositions that are not accessible to conscious experience. For the proponents of the computer metaphor, environmental data, whether originally encoded in verbal or visual form, constitute the input to the

Figure 7.22b. Miriam, a 7-year-old girl in the city school of Schwäbisch Gmünd, began her office building, which had a tiled, pointed roof, (above, left) from a frontal view and subsequently added the side view. The dotted picture frame of the drawing sheet served as a vertical line in this attempted perspective. The factory (above, center) was presented in side view only. It has windows with curtains, like all of Miriam's buildings except the church (above, right), which is marked by a big door and a clock in the gable. For the school (below, left), apartment building (below, center), and house (below, right), Miriam parsimoniously used the same form like a "stamp": a slender vertical building with a tiled, pointed roof. The three buildings differ only in the number of windows and, consequently, the number of stories.

deep propositional structure. There they serve in cognitive information processing to test hypotheses about the environment. Despite their polemics against the picture metaphor, proponents of the computer metaphor had to reintroduce the image as a picturelike and more detailed representation. In cognitive information processing, these have the function of making implicit propositional descriptions more explicit.

Support for the image theory came from the research of Soviet psychologists (Leontiev & Gippenreiter, 1966; Vekker (Wekker), 1966; Zaporozhets & Zinchenko, 1966). According to them, the image is a product of signal coding, which preserves the important geometric properties of the stimulus source. It is only because these geometric properties are preserved in the signal image that

Figure 7.23a. Güner was a 6½-year-old girl in the university school of Trabzon. She took advantage of the drawing task to render everything beautiful and full of flowers. The office (above, left) she showed from both the outside and, separately, from the inside, with the windows looking out. The factory (above, center) is reduced to a single-story home with television antenna. The mosque (above, right) was turned into a minaret with a flower on top. The school (below, left) has a flag and some pupils lined up outside. The two-story apartment building (below, center), has a flag, flowers flying in the air, and a big tree. The single-story house (below, right) features a chimney, a television antenna, and a tree next to it. Every building except the house was accompanied by a moon and at least one person, and two of them had a sun.

efferent motor activity can be applied efficiently to the properties of the stimulus source. Because the signal image is an icon of afferent information, it can mediate between afferent information from the stimulus source and the efferent action applied to it.

Soviet researchers have shown that such images are built up gradually in children when they actively explore an object by eye movement or touch. Thus the image was said to be a "motor copy" of the object. According to Piaget, children's drawings are a special case of imitation, where graphic forms are used to represent "internal models" (Luquet, 1927). Internal models are nothing other than mental images that have been stabilized by frequent internal imitation of perceptual activity. Hence, children's drawings should constitute an access to

Figure 7.23b. Amaya was a 6-year-old girl in the city school of Schwäbisch Gmünd. Amaya's parents came from Spain. She drew a multistory office (above, left) with a gabled roof. The factory (above, center), has few stories, but on the flat roof a thick chimney issues smoke. The church (above, right) features a clock in its gable and a cross on the roof. The school (below, left) was drawn in both frontal and side view at the same time, because Amaya tried to show it in perspective. The apartment building (below, center) is a multistory, rectangular building with a flat roof. Tenants peek out of every window. The house (below, right) has two stories and a gabled roof. Amaya's windows with small curtains and her doors are alike in all of her buildings.

the mental images on which they are based. If these images are undifferentiated, the drawing should be the same, if they are clearly articulated, the drawing should be clear as well (Basset, 1977). Globally, children's drawing ability develops in stages: from scribbling, to a phase of synthetic incapacity, continuing via intellectual realism ("the child draws what he knows"), to visual realism (Piaget & Inhelder, 1948/1967). Especially in the earlier phases of graphic activity, drawing and writing are not yet separated (Lurçat, 1979). In fact, both are based on graphemes, the smallest graphic elements, which develop between the ages of 4 and 6 years (Olivier, 1974). These graphemes constitute a sort of visual script that children use to note down their "internal models" on paper. The question is whether the development of graphemes and the development of drawing in global stages are "natural" and universal or whether they are influ-

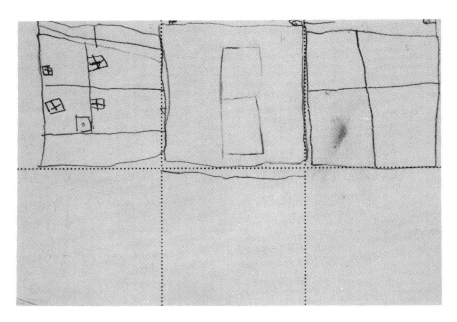

Figure 7.24a. Sinan, a 7-year-old boy in the village school of Cimenli, rendered the house (above, left), the apartment building (above, center), and the school (above, right) as squares secured by the coordinates of the drawing space. The squares were subdivided on the inside (house and school). The house features windows, and the school a Turkish flag. The mosque, factory, and office building were not drawn.

enced by culture. If drawing development in children consists of nothing other than constantly outgrowing the stock of drawing formulae present in their (sub-) culture, then the course of this development should vary from culture to culture (Wilson & Wilson, 1984). If this is not the case, then the findings on the development of general drawing ability and of graphemes should be capable of replication in very different cultures.

During the previous leg of our journey we dealt specifically with children's drawings of buildings. Building types such as the office, factory, religious building, school, apartment building, and house seem to be particularly suited for a study of natural and cultural factors in drawing development. Buildings are too complex to be easily described in words. Hence, they are best represented in drawings. They often vary from culture to culture and are, therefore, appropriate for finding out about cultural influences in children's drawings. They are also, with the exception of the house, not as stereotyped as are drawings of human figures or certain animals.

Figure 7.24b. Jürgen, a 7-year-old boy in the village school of Bartholomae, is in the same class as the girls Silke and Anna (see Figures 7.18b and 7.19b). Jürgen used the same "stamp" for all six building types: A front elevation with a gabled roof and a round window connected to a side elevation without a roof. The buildings were differentiated by a series of special features. The office (above, left) was depicted in terms of its activity—a desk with two little men, as in Anna's picture (see Figure 7.19b). In the drawing of the church (above, center), the front elevation turns into the steeple, and the round window into a clock. On the roof he placed a cross, and in the nave, two arched windows. In the factory (above, right), he showed a worker doing his job. The school (below, left) has two large windows and two small ones with shutters. The apartment building (below, center) was conceived of as a multistory building, as indicated by the balconies on the right. The house (below, right) has more windows than the apartment building, but no balconies. Both the apartment building and house have similar doors.

Some questions that remain open from previous studies on drawings of buildings have to do with factors that cannot be attributed to culture. In one study (Brucker, 1982) it was found that children suffering from cerebral palsy did not advance in their building drawings with the same pace of global drawing development as their nonhandicapped peers. If this was due to their handicap, one would expect the same retardation in their grapheme development. On the other hand, this retardation should not come into play in children of the same age from two different cultures. Their overall drawing development, as shown in their building drawings, should not be significantly different. There should also be no

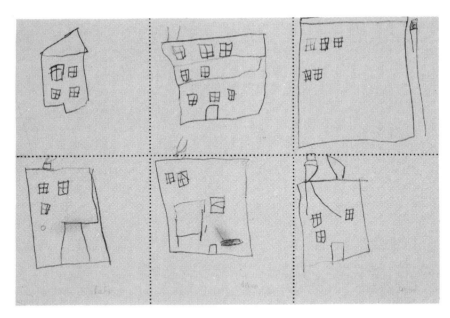

Figure 7.25a. Idris, a 6-year-old boy in the village school of Cimenli, drew all the buildings. The house (above, left) has two stories and a pointed roof. The apartment building (above, center) has three stories and a flat roof. The school (above, right) is distinguished by the flag. The factory (below, left) and the office (below, center) are similar flat-roofed, rectangular shapes. The mosque (below, right) has a minaret on top.

difference in their grapheme development (unless graphemes differ from culture to culture). Thus, general drawing development and grapheme acquisition is not expected to be cultural.

On the other hand, there are factors in children's drawings of building types that cannot be attributed to nature and must hence result from influences of the cultural environment. One study on building drawings seemed to indicate that there were no striking differences in the use of five distinctive features for the drawings of apartment buildings and houses between children of two cultures (Turkish and German), provided they were of the same age and came from the same sociogeographical (rural vs. city) background (Krampen, 1986b). The question remains whether this lack of difference between two cultures would also apply to other pairs of building types or whether the cultural specificity of some buildings would show up in drawings as one of the factors that could not be attributed to nature. Some qualitative observations seem to suggest the latter. In summary, we expect global drawing development along the four phases—for-

Figure 7.25b. Joachim, a 7-year-old boy in the village school of Bartholomae, was in the same class as Jürgen, Silke, and Anna. His office building (above, left) has a gabled roof and is "transparent." There are four people sitting in front of typewriters and four more waiting in the corridors on chairs. The flat-roofed factory (above, center) is spitting smoke from two chimneys. The church (above, right), with a clock and arched windows, bears a large cross on the steeple. The school (below, left) and the apartment building (below, center) have flat roofs, but the latter was drawn larger and has more stories. The house (below, right) was drawn with two stories, a gabled roof, and a chimney perpendicular to the roof line.

tuitous, failed, intellectual, and visual realism (Luquet 1927/1967; Piaget & Inhelder, 1948/1967)—and grapheme development as described by Olivier (1974) to be (1) "natural," (2) retarded in the handicapped, and (3) parallel in children from different cultures. Building types, however, should be drawn with different distinctive features if they do not look alike in two different cultural environments.

That such factors exist was shown by three studies on environmental influences. In the first (Ribault, 1965), children raised in an orphanage scored lower on a series of indicators of drawing development than those raised in their families. In the second (Krampen *et al.,* 1980), Turkish village children were less proficient in differentiating six building types in their drawings than their urban peers. In the third study (Krampen, 1986b), this difference between chil-

Figure 7.26a. Halim, a 7-year-old boy in the city school of Trabzon, drew a different number of stories for the office and factory (above, left and center). The office has a pointed roof, while the double factory buildings have flat roofs. The mosque (above, right) is a large dome with three tall minarets on top. The school (below, left), with a roof in pseudo-perspective and large windows, can be distinguished by the flag. The apartment building (below, center) has four stories and balconies on the roof. The house (below, right) has two stories and a pointed roof in pseudo-perspective.

dren from rural and urban schools was also found in Turkish and German children when they drew apartment buildings and houses.

Hypotheses of the Central Study

The glance backward brought to light some open questions that shall be answered by the empirical studies reported in the following part of this book. But before presenting the methods and results of these studies, I shall now formally express their hypotheses. Since it is not usual in the social sciences to express hypotheses in the affirmative, they are formulated here as null hypotheses. A null hypothesis maintains that there is no difference between the groups or factors involved in the study. Only if there is sufficient evidence to establish a difference between the groups or factors is the null hypothesis rejected. In the following

Figure 7.26b. Amir is a 6-year-old boy in the city school of Schwäbisch Gmünd. His parents are Turkish, but he grew up in Germany. Amir drew the office building (above, left) with three stories and a gabled roof. He gave the factory (above, center) a flat roof and two smokestacks. Amir drew a church (above, right) not a mosque. The church has a steeple with a cross, and windows with gothic arches. In drawing the school (below, left), Amir tried perspective, but failed. After using the eraser many times, he succeeded a little better with the perspective of the apartment building (below, center). The house (below, right), with a staircase window above the door, is shown in side elevation with a saddle roof.

study the empirical evidence will be regarded as sufficient to reject the null hypothesis if the statistical test indicates a probability of error as low as 5% (alpha = .05).

The null hypotheses formulated below will each be followed by an alternative hypothesis that could be tested if the first should fail.

First Hypothesis

The first hypothesis relates to the global phases of drawing development in children's drawings from two different cultures, those of Turkey and the Federal Republic of Germany (FRG):

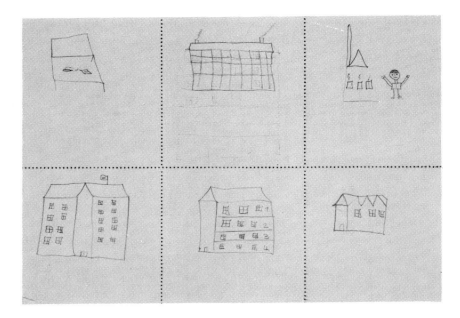

Figure 7.27a. Onur, a 7-year-old boy in the city school of Trabzon, showed the office (above, left) by drawing a table with some objects on it. The factory (above, center) is four stories and subdivided into many compartments. The mosque (above, right) features a minaret, dome, washing facilities, and a little man (Onur?). The school (below, left) of six stories is split into two halves by a pseudo-perspective. Again, there is a flag on the roof. The apartment building (below, center) has four stories (numbered inversely from 4 to 1) and was rendered almost in correct perspective. The house (below, right) has one story. Its perspective was hampered by the attempt to show the pointed roof from too many sides at the same time.

There is no difference between the drawings of different building types made by Turkish and German children between the ages of 3 and 12 when compared to the classical developmental phases defined by Luquet (1927) and Piaget and Inhelder (1948/1967).

If this null hypothesis is rejected, a possible alternative hypothesis could assert that the ratings of Turkish children's drawings indicate significantly slower progress in the development of drawing ability than those of the German children (or vice versa).

The test of the first hypothesis is aimed at finding out whether the phases of drawing development as outlined by Luquet and Piaget are universal (i.e., natural) or influenced by culture.

Figure 7.27b. Ingo was a 7-year-old boy in the village school of Bartholomae. Ingo's office building is "transparent." He shows a little person standing on a large chair in front of a desk with a lectern, telephone, and writing utensils. The factory building (above, center) has a hoisting crane on the roof and arched windows. The church (above, right) has a steeple featuring a clock, a cross, a chimney, and arched windows just like the factory. The school (below, left) and apartment building (below, center) differ in the number of stories and type of windows. The three-story school has windows filled with crossbars. The four-story apartment building has no crossbars in the windows. As in Onur's drawing of an apartment building, the stories are numbered from above to below (see Figure 7.27a). It is amazing that children from two different cultures arrived at so similar a conception of numbering the stories of an apartment building! The house (below, right) is marked by a gabled roof with chimney, few stories, curtains in the windows, and a garden fence.

Second Hypothesis

The second hypothesis concerns a comparison of grapheme development between cultures:

There is no difference in the graphemes used in the drawings of different building types made by Turkish and German children. Turkish and German children of this age span develop the same graphemes as those defined by Olivier

Figure 7.28a. Emin was a 7-year-old boy in the university school of Trabzon. His father works at sea, so Emin rendered the office (above, left) in the form of a large ship with a tiny building next to it. The factory (above, center) is a transparent square showing two people inside and a smokestack on the roof. The mosque (above, right) was represented by a round, closed form—the dome—and two vertical lines on it—the minarets—with the Moslem symbols on top. The school (below, left) is a transparent rectangle with one person inside, one outside, and a flag next to it. The apartment building (below, center) has four stories and a little man standing outside. The house (below, right) combines a pointed roof with three television antennas.

(1974) in his study of the drawings of French children. There is also no difference in the sequence of development of grapheme systems between Turkish and German children.

Should this null hypothesis be rejected, an alternative hypothesis could maintain that Turkish children did not use any of Olivier's graphemes in their drawings of buildings. Or, if they did use graphemes, these differed in form and sequence of development from those in the drawings of German children.

The test of the second hypothesis should establish whether Olivier's graphemes are universal (natural) or influenced by culture.

Figure 7.26b. Patrick, a 6-year-old boy in the city school of Schwäbisch Gmünd, drew the office building (above, left) with large windows. Through one of them you see a little man at his desk—a motif that he repeated in the factory drawing (above, center). The factory has a smokestack made out of bricks. Behind the factory gate, which closes the wall around the factory, a worker is standing. The church (above, right), with a steeple featuring a bell (in transparency), is decorated with stained-glass windows. In the school (below, left) two pupils are visible through the large windows. The large windows of the row of two-story apartment buildings (below, center) with three roofs and three chimneys also permits a look inside, and one sees the lamps hanging from the ceilings. The house (below, right) is three stories and simple.

Third Hypothesis

The third hypothesis has to do with the development of grapheme systems in physically handicapped and physically normal children:

The graphemes used by two groups from the same culture—one comprising physically handicapped children aged 6–12, and the other comprising physically normal children aged 3–6—are the same and develop in the same sequence.

Should this null hypothesis be rejected, an alternative hypothesis could

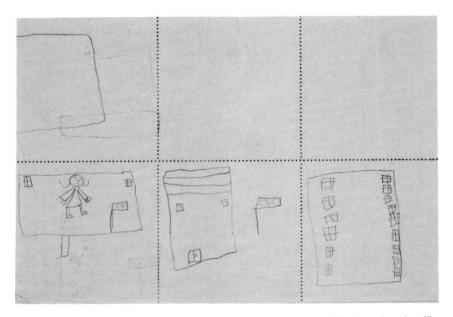

Figure 7.29a. Abdurrahman, a 6½-year-old boy in the university school of Trabzon, drew the office (above, left) as a simple square (before, he had tried a boat but erased it). He left out the factory and the mosque. The school (below, left) is a transparent rectangle with a female figure (the teacher?) and the flag inside. In place of an apartment building (below, enter) he drew a small house with two stories and the flag at the side, whereas instead of the house (below, right), he drew a rectangular building with many (6–9) stories and a flat roof. Perhaps Abdurrahman, who came from the country to the university school and is younger than his peers, got a little confused by the task of drawing so many different building types.

provide detailed answers to questions regarding the physical (natural) base of grapheme development.

Fourth Hypothesis

The fourth hypothesis concerns features in the graphic representation of different building types drawn by children from two cultures (Turkish and German):

Turkish and German children from the same age groups will use the same

Figure 7.29b. Türker was a 7-year-old boy in the city school of Schwäbisch Gmünd. His parents, too, came from Turkey, but he grew up in Germany (like Amir, see Figure 7.26b). His office (above, left) is a curtain-wall construction with a pointed roof. The factory (above, center) was drawn with a ruler. It features four smokestacks spewing smoke in garlands. The church (above, right), too, was drawn using a ruler. It has two steeples, one of which is topped by a cross. For the school (below, left), apartment building (below, center), and house (below, right), Türker used the same scheme: a pseudo-perspective. The school has a broader front with more windows (and curtains) than the apartment building or house. The school was also partially drawn with a ruler. Both the apartment building and house were drawn freehand.

distinctive features to represent a given building type. Also, there will be no significant difference in the distinctive features used to distinguish between different building types (such as office, factory, religious building, school, apartment building, and house).

An alternative hypothesis could claim that Turkish and German children from the same age group use different distinctive features to represent the same building type, or to distinguish between different building types (because they look different in their respective environments).

The test of the fourth hypothesis should help to distinguish between en-

Figure 7.30a. Zafer, a 7-year-old boy in the university school of Trabzon, drew a three-story office building (above, left). The factory (above, center), which spills its smoke over to the next drawing space, is an excellent portrait of the big Trabzon cement factory. The mosque (above, right) consists of two buildings with domes and a minaret. The school (below, left) with its large windows is, as usual, flanked by the Turkish flag. The apartment building (below, center) has three stories. Here you see that Zafer attempts, but has not yet fully acquired, perspective. The apartment block features many details typical of small apartment buildings, such as a door frame, door knob, and the difference in window form and size indicating a central staircase. The house (below, right) consists of two different volumes, each topped by a peaked roof. A pine tree was placed next to it, and a stylized sun is shining next to a single cloud. The overall coordination of the building dimensions is very advanced for age 7, although the office and the apartment building appear somewhat too small, the mosque and the house somewhat too big.

vironmental and cultural sources in children's drawings. At the end of this study, the tests for the four hypotheses should be able to tell us which influences in drawing development, grapheme development, and use of distinctive features are natural, and which are cultural, in the drawings of different building types made by children from different age groups and from two different cultures.

Figure 7.30b. Frank was an 8-year-old boy in the city school of Schwäbisch Gmünd. His office building (above, left) has a tiled roof with a television antenna. The three-story building is equipped with three letter boxes and three bell buttons. Above the door there is a sign saying "office" (in German: *Büro*). The factory (above, center) is a complex building with window bands and many smokestacks issuing thick clouds of smoke. The church (above, right) with its steeple and two crosses is presented with stained-glass windows and a decorated portal. The school (below, left) is marked, just like the office, by a sign spelling "school." But in contrast to the office, the school has curtains in the windows. The apartment building (below, center) is a glass curtain-wall structure of many stories. In contrast, the house (below, right) shows only two stories. There is a large garage door in the ground level of the house.

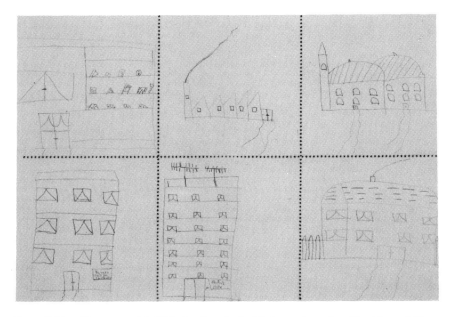

Figure 7.31a. Muazzez, a girl of 9 in the city school of Trabzon, shows the office (above, left) as a store with a display window that is completely out of proportion to the door. Her factory (above, center) features the typical sawtooth shed roof and a tall chimney stack. The mosque (above, right) is topped by domes and flanked by a minaret. The school (below, left) is one of the rare examples distinguished not by a flag but by a plate carrying the name of Muazzez's school in writing. The apartment building (below, center) is eight stories high, with two large TV antennas on the flat roof, and likewise bears a name plate. The house (below, right) has two stories and a smoking chimney on top of the roof. There are fence poles on both sides. The office, school, apartment building, and house feature the same curtains. The sizes of the buildings are not mutually coordinated. However, the roads issuing from the doors of the buildings were rendered in a primitive form of perspective, and the two buildings of the mosque are shown overlapping to indicate depth of space (although the overlapped building is somewhat larger in size).

Figure 7.31b. Janette was an 11-year-old girl in the city school of Schwäbisch Gmünd. She drew the office building (above, left) with five stories, half of it with glass curtain walls. The factory (above, center) features a shed roof and a large window band. Janette tried to draw the church (above, right) in perspective. On the peak of the steeple she put a weathercock, and on the roof, a cross. Inside the steeple you see the church bell in transparency. The school (below, left) is three stories with a gabled roof and two dormer windows. The apartment building (below, center) has four stories and a penthouse on top of the flat roof. The house (below, right) is a one-story bungalow.

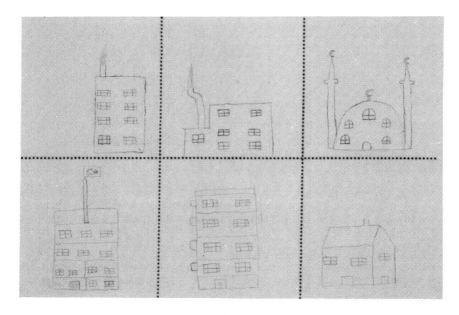

Figure 7.32a. Birol, a 9-year-old boy in the city school of Trabzon, drew a four-story office building (above, left) with a smoking chimney and a three-story factory (above, center) with a smoke-spewing bent tube. His mosque (above, right) is a dome flanked by two minarets, the three building parts each carry a crescent. The school (below, left) is four stories with the Turkish flag on top of the roof. The apartment building (below, center) is four stories high and features balconies protruding on one side. The house (below, right), rendered almost in correct perspective, is two stories high, with a smoking chimney on the pointed roof. Birol tried very carefully to keep the stories of the different buildings on one level and in proportion, although there is a small change of size between the buildings of the upper and lower rows. The effect is that size (number of stories) and special features (smokestack, dome, minaret, flags, balconies) easily distinguish the buildings in terms of their different functions (the office building perhaps less easily).

Figure 7.32b. Melanie was an 11-year-old girl in the city school of Schwäbisch Gmünd. Her office building (above, left) has only two stories, a flat roof, and a picture window on the ground-floor level. The factory (above, center) with three puffing smokestacks is a four-story box shape. The church (above, right) consists of a steeple with a clock, a cross, and the nave. The portal and windows feature round arches. The school (below, left) consists of two buildings. On the roof of the main building is a clock. The second building has larger windows than the first—representing perhaps a recent addition. The apartment building (below, center) is a five-story twin building, whereas the house (below, right) features only two stories and has a picture window like the office building. Melanie succeeded in keeping the buildings in proportion to each other.

Figure 7.33a. Ziynet, a 12-year-old girl from the university school of Trabzon, drew her five-story office building (above, left) with shops on the ground floor. The shop on the left of the entrance sells clothing for girls and boys, the one to the right, toys for girls and boys. The factory (above, center) was rendered with a sawtooth shed roof and furnished with two tall smokestacks bent at the top, each issuing a stream of smoke. The mosque (above, right) is very elaborate, with one main dome, five smaller domes and four minarets. The two-story school (below, left) has the usual flag next to it. The apartment building (below, center) is four stories high and somewhat resembles the apartment building on the university campus in which Ziynet lives. The house (below, right) has two stories and a large balcony on the first floor. Ziynet, too, tried to coordinate the sizes of the different buildings. The factory was perhaps a little small, but fully identifiable by other features. The doorsteps were handled well in perspective, also the sidewalk near the school, but not the road leading to the apartment building.

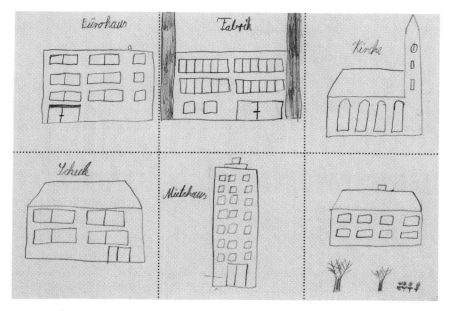

Figure 7.33b. Jürgen was a 9-year-old boy in the village school of Bartholomae. Jürgen drew a four-story office building (above, left) with a flat roof and broad windows. The factory (above, center) has three stories with horizontal window bands. It is flanked by two smokestacks. The church (above, right) is characterized by arched windows and a clock. The school (below, left) is marked by very large windows. The apartment building (below, center) is an eight-story tower with a penthouse on its flat roof. The house (below, right) has two stories and is situated in a garden with trees and flowers.

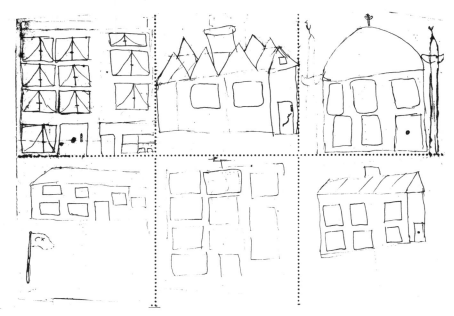

Figure 7.34a. Emin, a 12-year-old boy in the university school of Trabzon, drew a four-story office (above, left) with a store on the ground floor. All windows have the same curtains. The factory (above, center) features a shed roof and a big smokestack in the center. The mosque (above, right) is a two-story domed building flanked by two minarets. The two-story school (below, left) has a flag in front. The apartment building (below, center) has four stories and a flat roof with a television antenna. The two-story house (below, right) has a peaked roof topped by a chimney. To some extent, Emin tried (and successfully so!) to coordinate the sizes of the buildings. The large ones fill out the whole frame, the two-story ones do not. The attempt to draw the factory in perspective failed—it was too difficult. But the road leading up to the school was rendered well in perspective.

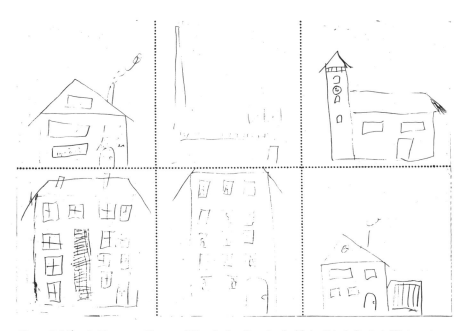

Figure 7.34b. Achim was a 12-year-old boy in the city school of Schwäbisch Gmünd. His two-story office building (above, left) with its pointed roof and broad window carries a sign with a name above the door. The factory (above, center) consists of a horizontally stretched building with a window band, a shed roof, and a tall smokestack. The church (above, right) was drawn with steeple and clock. The school (below, left) features four stories, a gabled roof, and a vertical staircase window. The windows are filled with crossbars. The five-story apartment building (below, center) with its gabled roof shows the tenants looking out of their windows. The house (below, right) has two stories and a pointed roof. It is flanked by a garage.

CHAPTER 8

Methods of the Central Study

General Remarks about the Methods Used

The central study of this book comprises two steps: first, the methods used in the study and, second, the results. This sequence is not only customary in scientific reporting but also logical, since the results of any study depend on the methods used in the investigation.

What should readers know about the methods of this study? First, they need to know both about the drawing task given to the children participating in this study and, second, about the children themselves. I will then explain how the drawings were observed and scored. To test the first null hypothesis—that the development in drawing ability is alike for Turkish and German children—drawing development was scored in keeping with the phases outlined by Luquet (1927) and Piaget and Inhelder (1948/1967). In order to test the second and third hypotheses, further criteria involved scoring graphemes during the ages of grapheme development in Turkish and German nonhandicapped and handicapped children. Finally, scores were also given for the distinctive architectural features used to distinguish between different building types. These three criteria—developmental, graphemic, and distinctive features—must first be analyzed for reliability. The question is whether these aspects of children's drawings can be reliably scored by the observers of the drawings. Once this question has been answered affirmatively, the data base of this study can be considered solid and can be analyzed statistically with respect to the absence (or presence) of group differences predicted by the four null hypotheses. These analyses involve three main techniques. The first is the preparation of phantom drawings, already summarily referred to in the context of Brucker's (1982) study on the drawings of handicapped children. The second determines the source of variance in the drawing data (i.e., is it a group difference due to age, building type, culture, etc?) using the technique of analysis of variance. Since this classical technique can only be applied to data fulfilling certain prerequisites of measurement, a third technique will be used on data that do not conform to these prerequisites. This technique, called "loglinear models," accomplishes the same purpose as analysis of variance in pinpointing sources of differences in the data.

The Drawings

The Turkish and German children participating in this study were all given the same task: to draw six different building types on a single sheet of paper (29.7 × 21.0 cm) that was subdivided into six squares. The building types were office building (O), factory (F), religious building (mosque or church) (R), school (S), apartment building (A), and house (H). All children were given graphite pencils in order to avoid the use of color as a variable.

The Children

The drawings of the 142 children participating in this study were selected from samples of previous studies (Krampen, 1986b; Krampen *et al.*, 1980)

Table 8.1. Age Distribution of the Children
Whose Drawings Were Used in this Study

Age (yrs)	Nonhandicapped		Handicapped
	German	Turkish	German
3	5	8	—
4	8	4	—
5	3	10	—
6	9	20	10
7	22	27	9
8	5	1	9
9	1	4	9
10	0	1	10
11	7	2	8
12	3	2	4
	63	79	59

n (nonhandicapped) = 142

carried out in the city of Trabzon (Turkey) and in the city of Schwäbisch Gmünd (southern Germany). In addition, the drawings from the Brucker (1982) study done by 59 handicapped children, most of them suffering from cerebral palsy, were used as a comparison group in a part of this study dealing with graphemes. The age distribution of the children is given in Table 8.1.

Previous studies (Krampen *et al.*, 1980; Ribault, 1965) had shown that the sex of the children did not significantly influence the results, at least as far as the variables used to differentiate between the different building types were concerned. Moreover, girls and boys were more or less equally represented in each age group. The sex of the children was, therefore, not included in Table 8.1.

Scoring the Observations on Children's Drawings

Global Rating Scores of Drawing Development

The first hypothesis of this study refers to potential differences in drawing development between Turkish and German children. An instrument for testing the significance of such differences was therefore needed. One way of devising a scale of this kind is by referring to peculiarities of the drawings themselves as Chen (1985) did for cube and cylinder drawings made by children of different ages. The instrument for the present study was constructed as follows: In reference to the four phases of drawing development proposed by Luquet (1927) and Piaget and Inhelder (1948/1967), a global rating of the drawing development in the building drawings was developed. Each of the 142 sheets consisting of six drawings was individually inspected for the occurrence of features indicated by Luquet and Piaget and Inhelder as typical for one of the four phases. Using this method, five groups of drawings with identical features could be identified. These, in turn, served as the basis for a 5-point rating scale (previously used in the Brucker [1982] study):

- First group (1 point): The drawing sheets do not contain a recognizable building in any one of the six subdivisions. Instead, scribbles or closed or open forms are featured. These sheets roughly correspond to the pre-figurative sensorimotor scribbling phase (fortuitous realism) of Piaget and Inhelder (1948/1967).
- Second group (2 points): The drawing sheets contain the first recognizable drawings of buildings and interiors in at least one of the subdivisions. Some of the six subdivisions still have scribbles or open or closed forms

instead of building drawings or interiors. These sheets might correspond to the stage of failed realism.

- Third group (3 points): All six subdivisions of the sheet contain recognizable building drawings with the following alternative restrictions:
  a. In addition to the building drawings, scribbles or open or closed forms are shown in some of the subdivisions.
  b. All six subdivisions are occupied by building stereotypes that cannot be differentiated according to their respective functions.
  c. The drawings feature buildings in which transparencies, pseudo-perspectives, or just interiors are shown. At the same time, however, there are some scribbles or open or closed forms on the sheet. These drawings mark a transition from the phase of failed realism to that of intellectual realism.
- Fourth group (4 points): The drawing sheets contain no scribbles or forms. All subdivisions of the sheet contain recognizable buildings. The first distinctions by secondary buildings (smokestack, minaret, steeple) or by requisite objects or symbols (cross, clock, flag) are made. On each sheet at least one of the six fields features either an interior, a transparency, or a pseudo-perspective. These sheets correspond to the phase of intellectual realism.
- Fifth group (5 points): The drawing sheets contain no transparencies or pseudo-perspectives in any of the six subdivisions. At least some of the building types are rendered in mutually proportional size (e.g., the house is smaller than the apartment building). Optionally, many realistic details are provided (e.g., bell buttons, tiles, etc.), or building stereotypes are approximated (e.g., factories featuring a shed roof). First perspectives, orthogonal, affine, or projective (Hagen, 1985) may appear but are not obligatory. These drawings represent the phase of visual realism.

Scoring of Graphemes

The second and third hypotheses of this study refer to the development of graphemes. Therefore, a method for scoring graphemes had to be devised. In accordance with the Olivier (1974) study, which claims that grapheme development takes place between the ages of 4 and 6, only the 67 drawing sheets of children aged 3–6 were used (42 Turkish and 25 German children). In addition, the 59 drawings from handicapped children between the ages of 6 and 12 in the Brucker (1982) study were examined. Since we know from this study that the global drawing development of handicapped children is retarded, the drawings of handicapped children aged 7–12 were also inspected for graphemes. For each sheet, the presence or absence of the three types of modulations and the 30 graphemes in the three grapheme systems defined by Olivier were scored regardless of frequency of occurrence. The scoring was facilitated by a scoring sheet containing the pictures of all grapheme forms. The point was to establish whether or not a grapheme occurred at a certain age.

Coding of Potential Distinctive Features

The fourth hypothesis of this study has to do with distinctive building features in children's drawings. Therefore, a method had to be designed that would allow us to identify these features. This method was developed as follows: Each of the six drawings on the drawing sheets was coded with respect to a total of 98 variables. Seven of these variables were demographic (e.g., nationality, sex, age), seven were directly related to known developmental phenomena (scribbles, forms instead of buildings, transparencies), and nine were related to nonarchitectural features in the drawings (presence of human figures, other objects, writing). The remaining 75 variables were potential distinctive building features (e.g., relative sizes of the six buildings drawn, in a rank order of building sizes; rated verticality/horizontality of the building shape; number of stories; presence of secondary buildings such as minaret/steeple or smokestack; form of roof; number, size rank, and verticality/horizontality of windows; presence of doors and architectural accessories such as stairs, chimneys, flags, clocks, TV antennas, and symbols). Each of the six drawings on a child's drawing sheet was scored on these 98 variables, yielding ($6 \times 98 =$) 588 measurements per child. For 142 children this meant collecting a total of 83,496 measurements.

Analysis of the Data

Analysis of the Global Ratings of Drawing Development

Reliability of the Global Assessment of Children's Drawings

Global assessment of the stages of drawing development in terms of ratings raises the question of whether such complex objects as children's drawings can be reliably scored. There have been some studies on the reliability of rating children's drawings. For instance, Martin and Damrin (1951) had 13 art students rate 31 drawings by children between the ages of 6 and 12 on 11 relatively complex variables. The students had to rate the drawings on such variables as: symmetry of the drawing as a whole, continuity of strokes, visible pressure of strokes, expansiveness of the drawing as a whole, degree to which the graphic elements were centered in the drawing as a whole, symmetry of individual figures in the drawing, sharpness and distinctiveness of the features in individual figures, clarity of position of natural features in individual figures, expansiveness of individual figures, and activity of individual figures. The coefficient of equivalence (Hoyt, 1941) between the raters on these 11 different measures ranged between .82 and .96, showing a large degree of agreement (1.0 would be the highest coefficient).

Since global ratings of the stage of drawing development constituted the data for testing the first hypothesis of this study, a special study of the reliability of these ratings was carried out. Three raters scored the same 17 drawing sheets of Turkish and German children of different age groups for drawing development using the 5-point scale described above. The sheets were chosen at random from the total sample of 142 children. The scores were cross-tabulated separately for the first and second, first and third, and second and third rater, and three Spearman Rho correlation coefficients were calculated to indicate the agreement between the pairs of raters. The general agreement among all three raters was subsequently assessed by calculating a coefficient of concordance (W).

Analysis of the Global Ratings with Respect to Sex, Age, and Nationality

The global ratings of the 142 drawing sheets were analyzed using the procedure of loglinear models. I will describe this technique in more detail below. It was used in this case to test the potential influence of the variables sex, age, and culture (Turkish, German) on the global rating score. I will show that this procedure successively eliminates all variables and interactions of variables that do not have a significant effect on differences in the data. In this case, the analysis should indicate whether the sex, age, or culture of the children (or any of their interactions) was responsible for any variance in global drawing development.

Analysis of the Grapheme Data

To analyze the sources of variance present in the grapheme data, three separate analyses of variance with the two most important variables, age and culture (and their interaction), were calculated. The data were the occurrence (or nonoccurrence) of the graphemes from each of the three grapheme systems reported by Olivier (1974) in the drawings of each child. In addition, the occurrence of scribbles, of the three kinds of modulations mentioned by Olivier, of letters, and of each individual grapheme was cross-tabulated for normally developing children aged 3–6 years ($n = 67$) and handicapped children aged 6–12 years ($n = 59$). Chi-square tests and analyses of variance were calculated to test whether the difference between the occurrence of graphemes in different age groups and the difference in the occurrence of graphemes between normally developing and handicapped children were due to chance or if they were statistically significant.

Analysis of the Distinctive-Feature Data

Reliability of Scoring

Like the global ratings of drawing development, the potential distinctive features of buildings in the drawings were also subjected to a study on scoring reliability.

In a previous study (Krampen *et al.*, 1980), the drawings of six building types made by 12 children chosen at random out of a total of 102 Turkish children had been scored by four raters on 26 architectural variables. An analysis of variance, with the raters comprising one possible source of variance in the data, had shown that they did not have any significant effect, whereas 8 of the 29 architectural variables in the drawings did.

But it seemed appropriate to assess scoring reliability in the present study with respect to the larger number of 75 potential distinctive architectural features in the children's drawings. Therefore, the six drawings by the same 17 children chosen at random for the reliability study of the global development ratings were also scored with respect to the 75 potential distinctive features by the same three raters. Mean relative frequencies of rater agreement or coefficients of concordance were calculated for each variable depending on the prerequisites of measurement fulfilled by the data.

Architectural Variables and the Phantom Drawings of the Different Building Types

In order to compare groups on the degree in which architectural variables are realized, average values had to be calculated. To see, for instance, whether

Turkish children from a certain age group drew, on the average, smaller factories than their German peers, the average sizes of factories would have to be compared.

Such measures were calculated for each of the 75 architectural features of the six building types. They are, of course, difficult to compare in numerical form. A visual form of data representation was therefore chosen. For each age group, the average values (median) of the most important architectural variables were taken to construct phantom drawings of the six building types. To construct a phantom drawing, the critical variables regarding the external shape and the internal articulation of the facade had to be defined. The external shape of a building drawing is determined (1) by its relative size in comparison with the other five building types (size rank), (2) its verticality or horizontality, (3) the presence or absence of a secondary building like a steeple or smokestack, and (4) the form of its roof. The internal structure of a building drawing is defined by (5) the number of stories, (6) the number of windows, (7) the relative size of the windows in comparison with those in the other building types, and (8) the verticality or horizontality of the windows. These eight variables constitute the main architectural features of a building drawing, without which a distinction between the various building types would be impossible. In fact, any drawing of a building comprises these variables.

These eight variables were used to construct "phantom drawings" of each of the six building types as follows:

The average (median) size rank of each building type was squared into a surface of a given size. This square was then transformed into the shape of a building type by using its average (median) verticality/horizontality rating. If the average shape was more horizontal, the square was transformed into a horizontal rectangle equal in surface to the square; if it was more vertical, it was transformed accordingly. The average number of stories (rounded to the next lower or upper integral) was then drawn into the average building shape. The average (median) number of windows was distributed over the stories. The size and shape of the windows were calculated in the same way as the size and shape of the buildings. Secondary buildings (minarets, steeples, smokestacks), roofs, and doors were added if their occurrence was statistically above chance. Tendencies in the occurrence of variables that were not statistically significant were indicated by dotted lines. In this way, each of the six building types for each group in the study could be visually documented in terms of size (relative to the others); average shape and form of roof; occurrence (or not) of additional secondary buildings; number of stories; and average number, size, and shape of windows.

Analysis of Variance of Variables concerning Relative Size

One of the most important architectural variables of the study is the relative sizes of the building types and their windows. These relative sizes should reflect the relative proportions for a given building type. Since both these variables are ranked in comparison with the other building types, their average (median) ranks cannot be taken as proportional in size to other buildings (e.g., one-half, one-third, etc.), but only as large or small in a hierarchical order. Such "ordinal" data could be treated by the Friedman two-way analysis of variance (Siegel, 1956), a technique applicable to these kinds of data. It was used to test for differences in the mean size ranks of buildings and windows. Since it could be presumed that window size depended in some way on building size, the measurements for both should rise or fall together. Correlation coefficients (rank and tau) were calculated to test this assumption.

Analysis by Loglinear Models

The technique of loglinear models permits the analysis of complex interactions between variables when these are expressed only in terms of frequency of occurrence in classes (e.g., Turkish/German, boys/girls, etc.). The term *loglinear* is meant to express that connections between these kinds of variables are rendered linear in scale (i.e., additive) by a logarithmic transformation. In the loglinear models technique, an extension of the chi-square test is applied. This test is normally used for assessing the difference between frequencies in two variables only (e.g., Turkish/German). But it also allows an examination of interactions between three or more variables with frequencies in classes (e.g., building type, culture, sex, etc.). These kinds of data are called nominal, since the classes can be named, but not brought into an obligatory order (ordinal), let alone be regarded as mutually proportional (interval). Basically then, the technique of loglinear models accomplishes for nominal data what analysis of variance accomplishes for data with a higher level of measurement (e.g., ordinal or equal-interval scaling). The 98 variables in this study are scaled on different levels of measurement—some on a nominal, some on an ordinal, and others on an equal-interval scale—and thus they cannot all be treated by analysis of variance. The technique of loglinear models fills this gap.

To define the loglinear models used here it is important to keep in mind that the main point of the present study is to investigate the role of the children's capacity to represent the environment by iconic rather than by verbal signs at different age levels. Moreover, the part culture plays in this process is to be defined. For reasons of practicability, the realm of the iconically coded environment has been reduced to architecture, more precisely, to different building types. The models of this study must, therefore, include the ages (A) of the children to test the development of iconic performance. They must also contain the six building types (B) to determine whether distinctions develop in their representations with increasing age. Finally, they must contain samples of subjects from (at least) two different cultures (C) to gauge the influence of culture in this process. The parameters of the model are, therefore; A (3–5, 6–7, 8–12); B (O, F, R, S, A, H); and C (T, G).

The data for each of the variables scored on the children's drawings can now be tested against the models to find out which of the three parameters or combination of them best fits the distribution of the data. The test of the models defines the discrepancy between *observed* frequencies in the class and frequencies *expected* according to the model. If the model is a tight fit, this discrepancy should be small; that is, it should not be significant.

This means that the distribution of each distinctive-feature variable scored in the study might be modeled best by variations either in age (A), or in buildings (B), or in culture (C), or by the combinations AB, AC, BC, or ABC.

Since a total of 98 distinctive-feature variables was scored for the six drawings of each child, the number of tests to be carried out would be very large.

It will be remembered, however, that the data were collected in different blocks. These blocks were:

- External demographic variables
- Known developmental variables in the drawings
- Nonarchitectural variables in the drawings
- Distinctive building features in the drawings

Table 8.2. Design of the Studies Employing Loglinear Models

Variables[b]	Model parameters[a]						
	A	B	C	AB	AC	BC	ABC
X	AX	BX	CX	ABX	ACX	BCX	ABCX
Y	AY	BY	CY	ABY	ACY	BCY	ABCY
Z	AZ	BZ	CZ	ABZ	ACZ	BCZ	ABCZ

[a]A, age; B, building type; C, culture.
[b]X, architectural; Y, nonarchitectural; Z, developmental.

Two of the demographic variables turned out to be model parameters—age (A) and culture (C). From each of the other three blocks of variables a selection was made, guided by the hypotheses of this study. Besides, a certain number of variables were not analyzed by the technique of loglinear models because thy had a higher than nominal level of measurement and could, therefore, be treated by other techniques. This meant that the number of variables to be tested using this technique could be reduced considerably. The design of the study with loglinear models is given in Table 8.2.

Table 8.2 shows the 21 possible models of outcomes on architectural, nonarchitectural, and developmental variables depending on age, building type, culture, or any combination of these. All 21 could be potential sources of variation in the data. The tightest fit of data to any one of the 21 models pinpoints the source responsible for differences in the data.

CHAPTER 9

Results of the Central Study

Global Ratings of Drawing Development

In the study on the reliability of globally rating the four stages of drawing development (fortuitous, failed, intellectual and visual realism), the coefficient of concordance between the three raters scoring the 17 drawing sheets chosen at random from the total of 142 was very high ($W = .9777$). This result shows that the procedure of globally rating the drawing development of children from two different cultures, when they are given the task of drawing the six different building types, is very reliable. This encouraging result gives the next step in the analysis a more solid grounding.

The analysis by loglinear models of the global ratings on the 5-point sale described in Chapter 8 was applied to all 142 drawing sheets of Turkish and German children. The analysis eliminated sex and nationality as insignificant factors of influence. Instead, a highly significant source of variance was the phases of drawing development as measured by the 5-point scale (chi-square = 53.83, 4 df, $p = .000$). In addition, age also proved to be highly significant (chi-square = 28.72, 5 df, $p = .000$). Moreover, the interaction of global ratings with age (chi-square = 103.85, 20 df, $p = .000$) was also responsible for variance in the data. In fact, if the frequencies of the five rating scores are tabulated against the age groups it can be seen that the older the children, the more frequently they receive high rating scales (Table 9.1).

Table 9.1 shows that the later phases of drawing development (e.g. intellectual and visual realism, with 4 and 5 points, respectively) go along with an increase in age. In conclusion, the results of the analysis of the global rating data do not permit a rejection of the first null hypothesis of this study. This hypothesis

Table 9.1. Frequency Distribution of Global Ratings
of Drawing Development by Age

Age (yrs)	Frequency per global rating score					Total
	1	2	3	4	5	
3	6	6	1	0	0	13
4	1	7	4	0	0	12
5	0	4	5	4	0	13
6	0	1	4	24	0	29
7	0	1	4	36	8	49
8–12	0	0	0	7	19	26
	7	19	18	71	27	142

maintains that there is no difference in the developmental phases of drawing ability between Turkish and German children. Drawing development scores, according to these data, are neither a function of culture (nationality) nor sex, but depend on age and its interaction with the phases of drawing development. In other words, drawing development depends on nature rather than on culture.

Graphemes and Grapheme Systems

Children from Two Different Cultures

An inspection of all the drawings of the 3- to 6-year-old Turkish and German children participating in this study shows that of the 30 graphemes listed by Olivier (1974), only three were never used by Turkish children (refer to section "Inventory of forms," Chapter 6, this volume, for explanation of the following symbols). These missing graphemes were $\bigcirc\bigcirc$ (= R + A + C + J) in the grapheme system G2, and $\diamondsuit$ (T + aA + C + S$_2$) as well as $\bigcirc$ (R + C + S$_3$) in system G3. In the drawings by the German children, only the grapheme $\diamondsuit$ (T + aA + C + S$_2$) from system G3 could not be found. This small number of missing graphemes might be due to chance or to the fact that these graphemes were not required for the task of drawing buildings.

The average number of graphemes per system that occurs at least once in any of the six drawings done by a single child is given for the different age groups and separately for Turkish and German children in Table 9.2.

By adding the numbers for the 6-year-olds in Table 9.2, you can see that Turkish children used an average of 12 at the end of grapheme development,

Table 9.2. Average Number of Graphemes from the Three Grapheme Systems
Used by Turkish and German Children

| | Average number of graphemes | | | | | | |
| | G1 | | G2 | | G3 | | |
Age	Turkish	German	Turkish	German	Turkish	German	n
3	3.50	3.60	4.12	3.80	0.25	0.00	13
4	4.25	3.75	4.50	5.00	0.75	0.87	12
5	2.80	3.33	5.70	3.68	1.40	1.67	13
6	3.20	3.00	4.95	4.89	4.20	5.00	29

while German children used approximately 13 of the 30 graphemes. This reduced application is due to the fact that the children in this study were not free to
draw what they wanted but were given the task of drawing buildings.

An analysis of variance taking into account the factors culture (Turkish,
German) and age as potential main sources of differences in the data shows no
significant differences for culture in the number of graphemes used by the children. There is also no significant difference for age within grapheme systems G1
and G2. A highly significant difference ($p = .000$) for age occurs, however, in
G3 (symmetrical graphemes). The reason for this increase can be seen in Table
9.2. Beginning with a very slow increase between the ages of 3 and 5, there is a
sudden rise in the occurrence of symmetrical graphemes at the age of 6. Since
culture is not a source of variance responsible for this increase, the grapheme
data for Turkish and German children were then pooled for a more detailed
inspection. The pooled data for the average occurrence of scribbles and modulations in different age groups are given in Table 9.3.

Table 9.3. Average Occurrence of Scribbles and Rotative
and Translative Modulations in the Drawings
of Turkish and German Children

| | | Modulations[a] | | | |
Age (yrs)	Scribbles	R	T	R + T	n
3	0.69	0.46	0.61	0.54	13
4	0.75	0.33	0.25	0.00	12
5	0.23	0.08	0.00	0.31	13
6	0.10	0.10	0.00	0.03	29

[a]R, rotative modulation; T, translative modulation.

As can be seen from Table 9.3, scribbles and modulations decrease steadily with age. A chi-square test calculated for the occurrence of scribbles indicates that their decrease with age is statistically significant ($p = .0003$, chi-square $= 24.447$, 6 df). The same test carried out for the number of rotative modulations was also significant ($p = .0237$, chi-square $= 9.465$, 3 df), as was the one for the frequency of translative modulations ($p = .000$, chi-square $= 28.181$, 3 df). Further tests showed that the decrease of combined rotative and translative modulations with age was equally significant ($p = .0002$, chi-square $= 19.624$, 3 df), as was that of all types of modulations taken together ($p = .0002$, chi-square $= 19.399$, 3 df). A comparison of Tables 9.2 and 9.3 shows clearly that in drawings of buildings, scribbles and modulations—the earlier forms of graphic activity—diminish as they are substituted by the three grapheme systems and almost disappear when symmetrical graphemes are produced by the children. This impressively confirms the data Olivier (1974) obtained with his own children and in his quantitative studies.

The data can be examined in more detail if you look at the increase or decrease of single graphemes. There is no significant evidence in the data that the occurrence of graphemes belonging to the earlier grapheme system (G1) decreases as the second system (G2) develops. Of system G1, it is only the slope $\wp$ (R + T + C) that diminishes significantly with age ($p = 0.269$, chi-square $= 9.183$, 3 df). This is probably because the children are now able to control the closure of the two ends of a round (R + C). On the other hand, there are two graphemes in system G2 whose occurrence increases significantly between the ages of 3 and 4 years. These graphemes are the irregular triangle $\triangleleft$ (T + A + C + J; $p = .0295$, chi-square $= 8.981$, 3 df) and the irregular quadrangle $\square$ (T + C + J; $p = .0357$, chi-square $= 8.563$, 3 df). The sharp increase of these two graphemes is probably due to the task of drawing buildings and might not occur as frequently in free drawings.

In comparison with systems G1 and G2, the increase in symmetrical graphemes (G3) between the ages of 5 and 6 years is quite apparent. Its occurrence is significant in the following graphemes:

$\wedge$	(T + aA + C + S_1)	$p = .0001$ (chi-square $= 20.339$, 3 df)
$\sqcap$	(T + O + J + S_1)	$p = .000$ (chi-square $= 30.007$, 3 df)
$\triangle$	(T + A + C + S_1)	$p = .0126$ (chi-square $= 10.848$, 3 df)
$\cap$	(R + T + A + O + S_1)	$p = 0.126$ (chi-square $= 10.848$, 3 df)
$\bigcirc$	(R + C + S_2)	$p = .0381$ (chi-square $= 8.421$, 3 df)
$\boxed{}$	(T + C + S_2)	$p = .0000$ (chi-square $= 26.295$, 3 df)
$\triangle$	(T + A + C + S_3)	$p = .0166$ (chi-square $= 10.242$, 3 df)

This selection of symmetrical graphemes appears to be useful in drawing buildings (e.g., the roof, the building shape, the door, etc.).

The tendency to combine letter writing with drawing starts to become noticeable at the age of 5, but it is not yet statistically significant.

In conclusion, the results of the analysis of the grapheme data do not permit the rejection of the second null hypothesis of this study. In fact, Turkish and German children between the ages of 3 and 6 show no significant differences in the graphemes they use or in the developmental sequence of the grapheme systems. Grapheme development, according to the data, is therefore not influenced by culture but depends significantly on age, that is, on maturation of the production end of the drawing activity. Once again it is nature rather than culture which determines drawing ability in children.

Physically Handicapped Children

To get further evidence in support of the hypothesis that the development of drawing ability is natural, the drawings of 59 physically handicapped children aged 6–12 years in the Brucker (1982) study were inspected. Again, the occurrence of the 30 graphemes listed by Olivier (1974) in the three grapheme systems was scored, as was the data from normally developing children. It was found that only two of these graphemes did not occur in the drawings of the handicapped. The missing graphemes are $\curvearrowright\!\cup$ (R + A + O) from system G2 and $\diamondsuit$ (T + aA + C + S_2) from system G3. A look at the graphemes of the normally developing children shows that $\curvearrowright\!\cup$ was found only four times in their drawings, while $\diamondsuit$ did not occur at all. Hence, with respect to the occurrence of Olivier's graphemes, there is no difference between the physically handicapped and normal children in this study. The average number of graphemes occurring at least once in one of the six building drawings of each handicapped child is given in Table 9.4 by age group and grapheme system.

Adding up the averages across the three grapheme systems for each age level you find that the average number of graphemes used by the handicapped children varies between approximately 8 and 10 graphemes. This number is clearly below the average of 13 graphemes used by the normally developing 6-year-old German children (see Table 9.2).

An analysis of variance using age as the main source of difference shows a significant decrease in the use of graphemes in G1 as the handicapped children grow older ($p = .031$). No such effect can be shown for G2 and G3, although there appears to be a tendency for symmetrical graphemes to increase after the

Table 9.4. Average Occurrence of Graphemes
from the Three Grapheme Systems Used
by Handicapped Children

Age (yrs)	Average number of graphemes			n
	G1	G2	G3	
6	4.10	4.70	0.60	10
7	3.11	5.44	0.56	9
8	2.89	5.33	0.33	9
9	2.11	4.67	1.11	9
10	3.20	5.70	1.40	10
11+	3.08	5.00	1.25	12

age of 8, when grapheme development is already concluded in the nonhandicapped child.

The average occurrence of scribbles and modulations in the drawings of the handicapped children is shown in Table 9.5.

By comparing Tables 9.3 and 9.5, it can be seen that handicapped children keep producing scribbles and modulations at a later age than their nonhandicapped peers. This suggests that the acquisition of the three grapheme systems is retarded in the handicapped by the persistence of more primitive modulations. But the most important difference between the handicapped and nonhandicapped children is the average number of symmetrical graphemes used.

Six-year-old handicapped children use an average of only 0.60 symmetrical graphemes as compared to the average of 5.00 used by their normally developing peers (cf. Tables 9.2 and 9.4). This difference is statistically significant at a very high level (t test, $p = .000$).

Table 9.5. Average Occurrence of Scribbles and
Modulations in the Drawings of Handicapped Children

Age (yrs)	Scribbles	Modulations[a]			n
		R	T	R + T	
6	0.60	0.30	0.10	0.10	10
7	0.66	0.55	0.22	0.11	9
8	0.33	0.22	0.11	0.00	9
9	0.22	0.11	0.00	0.11	9
10	0.10	0.20	0.10	0.00	10
11+	0.25	0.00	0.08	0.00	12

[a]R, rotative modulations; T, translative modulations.

The importance of this difference is confirmed if the 6- and 7-year-old handicapped children are pooled and compared with the normally developing 6-year-olds for each of the three grapheme systems. An analysis of variance with age as the main source shows no difference between the two groups for the grapheme systems G1 and G2. But there is a highly significant difference for the symmetrical graphemes of system G3 ($p = .000$). Such a difference persists in a comparison between handicapped children older than 7 years and their 6-year-old normally developing counterparts.

A series of comparisons between the age groups of handicapped and normal children is given in Table 9.6.

Table 9.6 shows that 6- to 7-year-old handicapped children range, with respect to the use of symmetrical graphemes, below the level of the 5-year-old nonhandicapped, while 8- to 9- and 10- to 12-year-old handicapped are below the level of 6-year-old nonhandicapped children.

A series of symmetrical graphemes frequently used by nonhandicapped children in their drawings of buildings is listed in Table 9.7, together with the frequencies of use in 6- to 7-year-old handicapped and 6-year-old nonhandicapped.

Table 9.7 shows that symmetry in graphemes used to draw buildings is achieved by handicapped children only in two cases. This explains, perhaps to some extent, the difference Brucker (1982) found between the global ratings of the handicapped's drawings of buildings and those of the normal children: The handicapped children simply did not develop the symmetrical graphic "building blocks" that are needed to draw buildings.

In conclusion, while there is no difference in the development of graphemes and grapheme systems between normal children of widely differing cultures, the

Table 9.6. Comparison of the Average Number of Symmetrical Graphemes Used by Physically Handicapped and Normally Developing Children of Different Age Groups

Age groups		4-year-old nonhandicapped	5-year-old nonhandicapped	6-year-old nonhandicapped
	Means	0.833	1.461	4.448
6- to 7-year-old handicapped	0.579	n.s.	$p=.05$	$p=.001$
8- to 9-year-old handicapped	0.722	n.s.	$p=.13$	$p=.01$
10- to 12-year-old handicapped	1.318	n.s.	n.s.	$p=.01$

Table 9.7. Comparison between Physically Handicapped and Normally
Developing Children in the Frequency of Use Made of Some Graphemes
Suitable for Building Drawings

| S-axes | Grapheme | Frequency | | Significance of difference |
		Handicapped 6- to 7-year-old children	Nonhandicapped 6-year-old children	
1	⌐¬	21	76	.000
1	/\	10	69	.000
1	△	0	31	.05
1	∩	0	31	.05
2	▭	0	72	.000
2	○	0	34	.05

null hypothesis that claims there is no significant difference between physically handicapped and nonhandicapped children of the same culture must be rejected. There is an important difference between the two groups when it comes to their capacity to use symmetrical graphemes. This finding once again suggests that grapheme development is an ontogenetic universal connected with the maturation of muscles and the acquisition of a skilled eye-hand coordination that is retarded in physically handicapped children. If one follows the literature on the influence of impairment on drawing ability it becomes evident that the reason for this retardation is the distorted kinesthetic perception of the body axes in handicapped children. It is rendered asymmetrical by physical damage, and symmetry has to be learned slowly in a more abstract way and perhaps through special training in a school for the handicapped. I want to suggest that the "general difficulty in drawing" that Abercrombie and Tyson (1966) found in children with cerebral palsy is in fact a "general difficulty with body symmetry."

Distinctive Features of Different Building Types

The Main Distinctive Features

The main distinctive features used by both Turkish and German children to differentiate between the six building types were employed to construct phantom drawings (refer to "Analysis of the Data," Chapter 8, for explanation of phantom drawings). These features are listed here with their coefficients of scoring reliability (excepting the relative size of building, shape and windows):

- Relative size of building shape in comparison with others (size rank)
- Verticality versus horizontality of the building shape ($W = .91$)
- Form of the roof (average relative frequency of scorer agreement ranging between 75.3 and 99.2)
- Presence or absence of secondary buildings, such as smokestack, minaret, steeple (average relative frequency of scorer agreement = 87.93)
- Number of stories ($W = .91$)
- Number of windows ($W = .96$)
- Relative window size of a building type in comparison with the others (size rank)
- Verticality versus horizontality of windows ($W = .82$)

In addition, the following variables played a role in differentiating the building types:

- Presence or absence of door(s) (average relative frequency of scorer agreement = 83.75)
- Presence or absence of symbols (flag, crescent, cross, etc.) (average relative frequency of scorer agreement = 93.04)

As can be seen from the list, scorer agreement is high (ranging between 75.3 and 99.2). A number of other variables, concerning secondary architectural features (e.g., roof tiles) or features in the surroundings of the drawing (e.g., plants, vehicles, etc.), were not considered as distinctive of building types in this study. Using these 10 distinctive features for differentiating building types in their drawings, both Turkish and German children of different age groups went about their drawing task. My contention is that different uses of these distinctive features mark, as a rule, a difference in the mental image reflecting an environmental and cultural influence.

Two Orders of Phantom Drawings

The phantom drawings constructed for the different age levels in the two cultural groups can only be read by keeping in mind the main distinctive features. The drawings can be ordered in two ways: they can be arranged according to age level and presented in the sequence in which the children were instructed to draw them (office, factory, church, school, apartment building, house); or they can be presented according to building type, showing the development of each type through three different age levels (3–5, 6–7, 8–12 years), which roughly correspond to the phases of drawing development of Luquet (1927) and Piaget and Inhelder (1948/1967). In the first case, we have what might be called "idealized" drawing sheets for the different age levels of the two cultural groups. In the second case, we follow the "developmental career" of each building type in the two cultural groups. Each case offers a different look at the same data and will therefore be presented extensively; first the idealized drawing sheets, then the developmental career of the building types. The descriptions of the phantom drawings should draw our attention to the crucial differences between age and cultural groups.

The "Idealized" Drawing Sheets

The Idealized Drawing Sheets of Children 3–5 Years Old

Turkish Children 3–5 Years Old

In the drawings of the youngest Turkish children (Figure 9.1), "failed realism" with its scribbles and simple forms prevails. Only the factory, apartment building, and house are drawn on a level above that of chance. The most striking distinctive feature of the external shape of the buildings seem to be

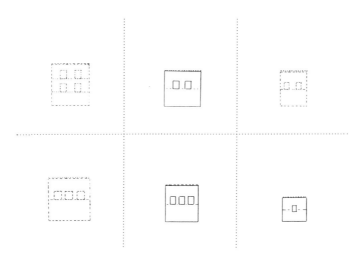

Figure 9.1. Idealized drawing sheet of 3- to 5-year-old Turkish children.

nondimensional size (e.g., the small house is pitted against the big apartment building). Verticality versus horizontality of the house shape does not yet play an important role. Neither does the form of the roof play a role in differentiating the building types. Also, neither factory nor mosque are furnished with their secondary buildings—smokestack and minaret.

Looking at the facade structure of the building shapes, you find that all tend to have two stories, except for the office, which has three. The number of windows ranges from two to four, and window size seems to depend on the size of the building. None of the buildings has a door. Conventional signs (e.g., the flag with crescent) are not yet used to distinguish different building types. It must be concluded that at the age of 3 to 5 years the Turkish children cannot yet clearly distinguish the six building types in their drawings. This inability must, at least in part, derive from incomplete mental images due to insufficient environmental exposure.

German Children 3–5 Years Old

In the drawings of the German children (Figure 9.2), "failed realism," indicated by scribbles and forms, must be attested for five of the six building types: no building type was rendered with a significant frequency, with the exception of the house depicted as a triangle. If the few existing building drawings are compared, then, as in the case of the Turkish children, nondimensional

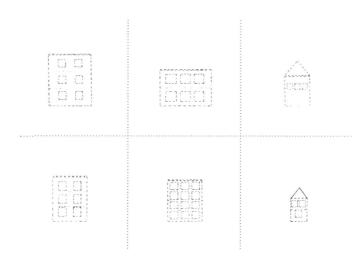

Figure 9.2. Idealized drawing sheet of 3- to 5-year-old German children.

size of the shapes is the most obvious distinctive feature: the house is tiny, and all other buildings are huge in comparison. Like their Turkish peers, German children made the house and the religious building smallest. There also seems to be some attempt to distinguish the factory from all the other buildings that have a vertical shape by using horizontality. If drawn, the church and house show a pointed roof, the church as a tendency, and the house always given in triangular form. Again we find no smokestack in the factory drawings and no steeple in the church drawings. Unlike the Turkish children of this age, the German children tend to differentiate buildings by the number of stories and windows. If drawn at all, the factory, church, and house have only two stories. No building is drawn with a door. There are no symbols used (e.g., the cross). In conclusion, the German children aged between 3 and 5 years do not really distinguish between the different building types in their drawings.

The parallels with Turkish children of the same age lends further credit to the theory of incomplete mental images.

The Idealized Drawing Sheets of Children 6–7 Years Old

Turkish Children 6–7 Years Old

At this age, the Turkish children draw all building types with significant frequency (Figure 9.3). Dimensional size (i.e., the idea of "larger than" and "smaller than") begins to be used as a means of distinguishing the buildings. The house and mosque are smallest, and the apartment building and school are the largest. The house and school have a saddle roof. The mosque is a tendency drawn with a dome. Factories seldom show a smokestack, but mosques tend to have a minaret. The apartment building is distinguished from all the other buildings by its four stories and large number of windows. The mosque and house have the fewest windows. The mosque sometimes has vertical windows as a distinction. Only the office and the factory are without doors. The school is regularly distinguished by the Turkish flag with crescent—as is usually the case in Turkish reality.

It is at elementary school age then that the Turkish children begin to use many of the architectural features and symbols to differentiate building types in their drawings. The fact that the school is the biggest building in the drawings might be explained by the salience this building has for children of this age. Unfortunately, the phantom drawings cannot show the transparencies and pseudo-perspectives characteristic of "intellectual realism" in the drawings of

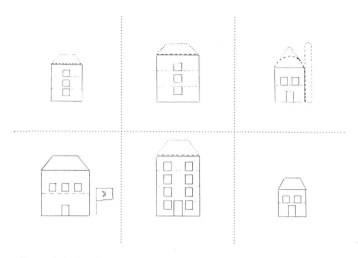

Figure 9.3. Idealized drawing sheet of 6- to 7-year-old Turkish children.

this age group. At this age the mental image of the different building types seems to be complete, but difficulties with perspective and vantage points shape the inconsistencies in the drawings. Also, environmental and cultural influences begin to appear, as in the case of the dome in the drawings of the mosque.

German Children 6–7 Years Old

As in the drawings of their Turkish peers, all building types are shown with significant frequency by the German children between the ages of 6 and 7 (Figure 9.4). Here, too, dimensional size has become a significant distinctive feature, setting the large school building (obviously relevant for this age group) apart from the small house. Verticality is significant for the high apartment building, office, and school. Horizontality appears significantly often in the long factory and the shorter shape of the church's nave. For the German children of this age group, the house still tends to have a pointed roof, whereas the office, church, school, and apartment building tend to feature saddle roofs. This often gives rise to pseudo-perspectives in the individual drawings. The factory, regularly, and the apartment building, frequently, have flat roofs. Factories are regularly accompanied by smokestacks, churches by steeples. Offices and apartment buildings feature four stories, the factory, the church, and the house are given two. The office, school, and apartment building have the most windows, the church and house the least. The school tends to have the largest windows of all. The church

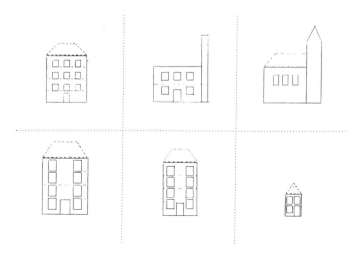

Figure 9.4. Idealized drawing sheet of 6- to 7-year-old German children.

windows are the most vertical, although windows seem to be drawn vertically for some of the other buildings (office, school, apartment building) by the German children of this age. Every building now regularly has a door. Churches are sometimes distinguished by a cross or a clock, a clear indication of cultural influence in the images. Individual drawing show, of course, many transparencies and pseudo-perspectives, which cannot be rendered in phantom drawings.

The "Idealized" Drawing Sheets of Children 8–12 Years Old

Turkish Children 8–12 Years Old

In this age group, the marks of "visual realism" become evident. In fact, a "correct" perspective appears with significant frequency in the case of the house (Figure 9.5). The office, mosque, and apartment building have now become the largest buildings, while the house and factory are the smallest. The decrease in the size of the factory is surprising and might be explained by the rare occurrence of factories in the environment of the Turkish children who participated in this study. The office, school, and apartment building definitely have a vertical shape, while the factory, mosque, and house are clearly horizontal. The roof of the mosque is regularly dome-shaped, the apartment building has a flat roof, and

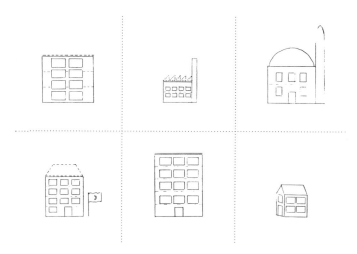

Figure 9.5. Idealized drawing sheet of 8- to 12-year-old Turkish children.

the house a saddle roof in perspective. The factory and mosque are always accompanied by their secondary buildings—the smokestack and the minaret. The building with the most stories is the apartment building. The factory and mosque are two-story buildings. The school and apartment building have the largest number of windows. In keeping with its size, the office building has the largest windows. In this oldest group of children, the mosque is the only building with vertical windows. The windows of all other buildings are now horizontal. Doors are drawn on all buildings (not shown on office and factory due to lack of space). The school is marked by the Turkish flag. With the exception of the factory, the buildings seem to be rendered in a mutually proportional size, and the number of windows begins to approach a realistic estimate. These are indices of mental images adapted to the environment as it is experienced daily.

German Children 8–12 Years Old

"Visual realism" becomes equally evident in the drawings of the German 8- to 12-year-olds (Figure 9.6). For no building type, however, is perspective used with significant frequency as yet. The apartment building is now the largest building, the house the smallest. The apartment building remains the only vertical building—all others are horizontal. Among these buildings the factory has

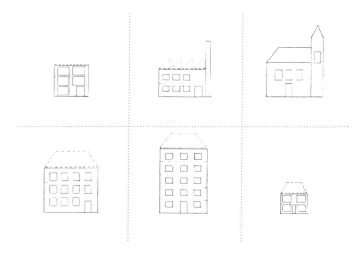

Figure 9.6. Idealized drawing sheet of 8- to 12-year-old German children.

the most horizontally elongated shape. The church is the only building in which the roof is clearly gabled. For all other buildings, only tendencies toward different roof forms could be found. Smokestacks and steeples are featured regularly as secondary buildings in factories and churches. The apartment building has the most stories, the house and church have the least. The apartment building also has the largest number of windows, followed by the school; the house has the fewest. While the office has the largest windows, the apartment building is represented with the smallest. Church windows are vertical, the windows of all other buildings are horizontal, especially those of the office and house. The buildings seem to be mutually in proportion, although the largeness of the apartment building and the smallness of the house appear somewhat exaggerated at first glance. The smallness of the office building is compatible with the factual situation in a small German town such as Schwäbisch Gmünd, where, on the other hand, high-rise apartment buildings also are present.

In conclusion, both groups of 8- to 12-year-old children seem to derive their drawings from complete and detailed mental images. At the same time, differences in the cultural environments in Turkey and southern Germany can be inferred from the drawings.

After having looked at the six building types to compare age groups, the "developmental career" of each building type will now be studied separately.

The "Developmental Career" of Six Building Types

The Developing Image of an Office Building

The Office Building in the Drawings of Turkish Children

In the office drawings of the youngest Turkish children (aged 3–5, nursery school), "failed realism" with scribbles and simple forms prevails (Figure 9.7, top). In fact, the office building is not drawn with significant frequency in this age group. If drawn at all, it is a vertical building with three stories, a flat roof, a median number of four windows, and no door.

Between the ages of 6 and 7 years, the building shape shrinks in size, is reduced to two stories with a median number of three windows, which are smaller in size, and still has no door.

At the ages of 8 to 12 years, the office building attains its final form as a very large, vertical four-story building with a median number of eight large horizontal windows. By this time, it is always drawn with a door (not shown due to lack of space). The roof has a very strong tendency to be flat.

During the three phases of age, the size and the number of stories and

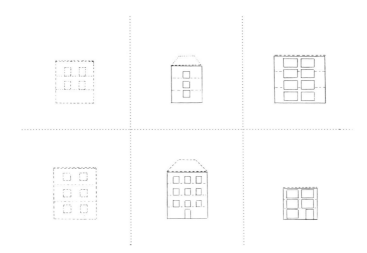

Figure 9.7. Development of the image of an office building for Turkish (top) and German (bottom) children.

windows of the office building develop in the form of a U-shaped curve. The dip in size as well as number of stories and windows is probably due to the high number of transparencies that have been found in the office drawings of this study. In fact, the office building was more often drawn as a transparency or a furnished interior by the Turkish children aged 6–7 years than any other building. This shows that the office building is known more for its internal activities than its external appearance.

The Office Building in the Drawings of German Children

Like their Turkish peers the youngest German children (aged 3–5, nursery school) fail to draw the office building with significant frequency, using scribbles and forms in its place (Figure 9.7, bottom). Whenever they draw the office it tends to be larger than the other buildings. Vertical in shape, it has three stories with a median number of six windows and no door.

At the ages of 6 to 7 years, the office is still vertical, but it has decreased in size, augmented in stories and number of windows, is drawn with a door, and tends to have a saddle roof.

By the ages of 8 to 12 years, the final form of the office building is very small in size, horizontal in shape, with a tendency for the roof to be flat. A median number of five very large horizontal windows is distributed over three stories.

There is a striking decrease in size over the three phases of development. Also the number of windows is smallest in the last phase.

The office building seemed to present similar conceptual difficulties to the German children as it did to the Turkish. It was the building type that showed more transparencies than any other building, which indicates that the children's mental image of an office building is not much shaped by a building form but by their experience of what happens inside.

The Developing Image of a Factory

The Factory in the Drawings of Turkish Children

The factory is drawn by the youngest Turkish children with significant frequency as a large, square-shaped, two-story building with a few (median two) windows and, more often, with a flat roof (Figure 9.8, top). It has no smokestack or door.

By the ages of 6 to 7, it has increased in size, the number of windows has

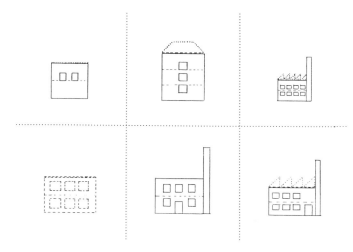

Figure 9.8. Development of the image of a factory for Turkish (top) and German (bottom) children.

increased slightly, and sometimes a smokestack has been added. The factory still has no door.

In the final phase of development, between the ages of 8 and 12 years, the factory is radically diminished in size, has clearly become a horizontal building with a tendency toward a flat or a shed roof, and is regularly accompanied by a smokestack. At the beginning and end of its development the factory remains two-storied. The number of windows increases strongly in the last stage. The windows are very small and horizontally extended.

On the whole, whereas the factory decreases in size, the tendency toward a flat roof remains, the windows augment in number but decrease in size and verticality. For an explanation of this development it should be remembered that in the Turkish city of Trabzon there was only one, albeit very impressive, factory, producing cement for the whole region. This factory was portrayed by some of the children. It looked like Zafer's drawing (Figure 7.30a).

The Factory in the Drawings of German Children

The factory is not drawn with significant frequency by the youngest German children, who often use scribbles and forms instead. If drawn at all, it frequently features a two-story horizontal shape with a median of six large, square windows (Figure 9.8, bottom). The roof tends to be flat, and there is no smokestack.

In the drawings of the 6- to 7-year-old German children, the shape decreases in size but remains horizontal and has a flat roof. It is regularly accompanied by a smokestack. The number of stories (two) and the windows (six) remains the same as in the few drawings of the youngest group, although the size of the windows decreases. A door is regularly drawn.

At the ages of 8 to 12 years, the factory remains approximately the same size but is more horizontal in shape. The roof tends to be flat or shed and, as a rule, features a smokestack. The number of windows remains the same (a median of six), and the size of them is still small, but the design has definitely changed to a horizontal format. The factory is always drawn with a door. Factories are more frequent in the environment of the German children in this study—even in the more rural area of Bartholomae. Building up a mental image of a factory should, therefore, have been easier for the German children than for their Turkish peers.

The Developing Images of Two Types of Religious Buildings

The Mosque in the Drawings of Turkish Children

The youngest Turkish children do not draw a mosque with significant frequency. In the few drawings of mosques they make, the building has a vertical shape and two stories with two vertical windows (Figure 9.9, top).

At the ages of 6 to 7 years, the size of the mosque decreases somewhat but the verticality remains. The roof is now tendentiously drawn as a dome or is

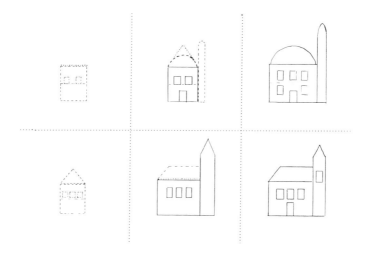

Figure 9.9. Development of the image of a religious building for Turkish (top) and German (bottom) children.

pointed, and there is a definite tendency to add a minaret. The number of stories and windows remains constant, and windows stay vertical. A door is now shown regularly.

By the ages of 8 to 12 years, the mosque increases considerably in size. The body of the building has become slightly horizontal. It is still topped by a dome, and a minaret is now added regularly. The number and size of the windows has increased, but they remain vertical throughout the three phases of development. On the whole, whereas the mosque increases in size and number of windows, the image of it as a two-story building with vertical windows remains constant throughout the three phases. Obviously, the presence of the dome and minaret in the image can only be explained as culturally determined architectural features in the environment of Turkish children.

The Church in the Drawings of German Children

The church is not drawn by the youngest German children with significant frequency. If drawn at all, it is given a small, two-story vertical shape with a median of three square windows and frequently a pointed roof (Figure 9.9, bottom). No door is drawn.

At the ages of 6 to 7 years, the building shape has increased in size and become horizontal. A steeple is added regularly. The roof tends to be either flat or gabled. The number of windows remains at three and they are now clearly vertical. But the door is still not drawn with significant frequency.

For the 8- to 12-year-old group, the church has remained approximately the same size, but the nave has become even more horizontal in shape. The roof is now decidedly gabled. The two stories remain throughout all three phases. The number of vertical windows has increased, but his is due to windows in the steeple. A door is now featured regularly. As in the case of the mosque, the image of a two-story building with vertical windows has remained constant. From the first to the third phase it has increased in size, and the building is now horizontal with a gabled roof and a steeple. The nave and steeple are the constant features of the church in the drawings of the older German children—a clear indication of cultural influences on the image from which they are derived.

The Developing Image of a School

The School in the Drawings of Turkish Children

The school was not drawn with significant frequency by the 3- to 5-year-old Turkish children. When drawn, it is a large, almost square, two-story building

(Figure 9.10, top). The roof tends to be flat. There is a median of three fairly large and almost square windows. The school has no door and is not yet marked by a Turkish flag.

At the ages of 6 to 7, the building increases in size and takes on a square shape with a gabled roof. Three fairly large square windows are distributed over the facade. A door is drawn regularly, and almost every school drawing shows a Turkish flag (either next to the building or on the roof).

In the last phase of development, the school decreases in size and increases in verticality. The roof still tends to be gabled. The number of stories doubles, and the median number of windows increases to 10. These windows have decreased in size and are now slightly horizontal. The school is furnished with a door and is always accompanied by a Turkish flag. As for size, the school develops in an inverted U shape during the three phases—first increasing, then decreasing. In contrast, the number of stories increases, and with it the number of windows. It would seem that there is no particular architectural feature identifying the school building for the Turkish children; instead, a nonarchitectural sign is used—the Turkish flag, which is in fact an obligatory feature in all schools in Turkey.

The School in the Drawings of German Children

The youngest German children in this sample did not draw the school building with significant frequency. The existing drawings indicate a relatively

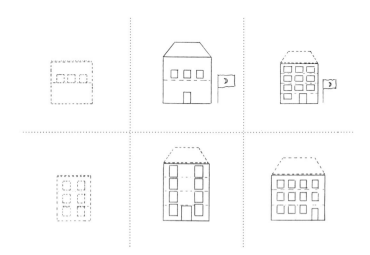

Figure 9.10. Development of the image of a school for Turkish (top) and German (bottom) children.

small, vertical, three-story building (Figure 9.10, bottom). Many small, square windows (a median of seven) are distributed over the stories, but there is no door.

By the ages of 6 to 7, the school has increased in size but still maintains its vertical shape and has a tendency toward a gabled roof. Many vertical windows are distributed (a median of eight) over its four stories. A door is now drawn regularly.

In the final phase of development, the school decreases only slightly in size but becomes horizontal. The roof still tends to be gabled. A median number of 11 square windows is spread across the three stories and the building is furnished with a door.

In conclusion, the school keeps a basic three- to four-story scheme and tends to have a gabled roof. Its number of windows increases during the three phases. The most important change is the development from a vertical to a horizontal shape in the drawings of the oldest group.

The Developing Image of an Apartment Building

The Apartment Building in the Drawings of Turkish Children

The apartment building is drawn with significant frequency by the youngest group of Turkish children (Figure 9.11, top). It is a large square, two stories high, and features a median number of three large, square windows. The roof tends to be flat and there is no door.

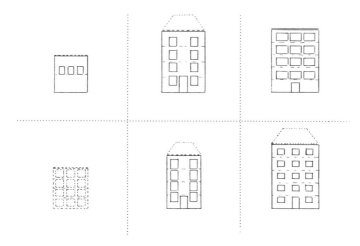

Figure 9.11. Development of the image of an apartment building for Turkish (top) and German (bottom) children.

With the 6- to 7-year-olds, the apartment building keeps its large size, but the shape has become vertical. The tendency toward a flat roof or gabled roof persists. By now it has four stories with a median number of eight large, square windows. A door is drawn regularly.

In its final form, drawn by children of 8 to 12 years, the apartment building has once more increased in size. It remains vertical and regularly has a flat roof. The number of stories has increased to five, the number of windows to a median of ten. These windows are large and horizontal. The apartment building is always drawn with a door.

In summary, the apartment building augments in size and verticality, and its roof becomes flat. The number of stories and windows increases, and the windows get larger in size and finally become horizontal.

The Apartment Building in the Drawings of German Children

The youngest German children (3–5 years) do not draw the apartment building with significant frequency. The existing drawings show a large, vertically shaped building of four stories with 12 large, square-shaped windows (Figure 9.11, bottom). The roof tends to be flat, and there is no door.

By the age of 6 or 7, the shape of the apartment building has somewhat decreased in size but has become more vertical. There is still a tendency for the building to have a flat roof, but gabled roofs are also drawn frequently. The number of stories is still four, the number of windows has decreased to a median of eight, and there is always a door.

In the drawings of the 8- to 12-year-olds, the apartment building is very large. It remains vertical but has developed a tendency toward a gabled roof. The number of stories has increased to five, the number of windows to a median of fifteen. The windows are small in size and stretched horizontally. The apartment building is always drawn with a door.

In conclusion, it appears that during the three phases, the apartment building is always conceptualized as large, vertical, with many stories, and many windows.

The Developing Image of a House

The House in the Drawings of Turkish Children

The 3- to 5-year-old Turkish children drew the house with significant frequency as a small square shape with two stories and one small window (Figure 9.12, top). The house tends to have a flat roof, and there is no door.

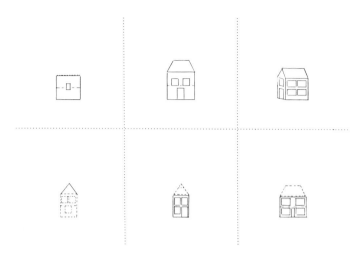

Figure 9.12. Development of the image of a house for Turkish (top) and German (bottom) children.

By 6 to 7 years of age, the house is still a small square shape, but the roof has become gabled. The number of stories remains at two, and there are two windows which have increased in size. There is always a door.

In the third phase of its "developmental career," the house is still small but has now become horizontal. Turkish children of 8 to 12 drew a gabled roof significantly often and in perspective. The number of stories is between two and three. A median number of five large and horizontally stretched windows are distributed over the facades. All houses feature a door.

In summary, the small size of the house is maintained in all three phases of its development. But there is a change in shape from the more vertical toward the horizontal. The roof develops from being flat to gabled and is finally drawn in correct perspective. The number of stories stays at an average of two. But the number of windows increases as they become larger is size and are drawn horizontally.

The House in the Drawings of German Children

The youngest group of German children did not draw the house with significant frequency. But the form of a triangular, peaked shape was drawn with significant frequency for the house (Figure 9.12, bottom). In the existing house drawings, it is often represented as a small vertical, two-story shape with a median number of three small, square windows. The roof tends to be peaked. Most of the time there is no door.

At the ages of 6 to 7, the small house has become even tinier. It is still vertical and, as a tendency, topped by a peaked or saddle roof. It still has two stories with three windows. Windows are somewhat larger and more vertical than in the antecedent phase. A door is almost always drawn.

At the ages of 8 to 12 years, the house is still small but is now horizontal. It tends to feature a gabled roof and four large horizontal windows. There is always a door.

In conclusion, the small size of the house is kept in all three phases of development. But the shape changes from vertical to horizontal. The roof changes from a tendency to be peaked to being gabled. The two-story scheme is maintained, as is the small number of windows. The size of the windows increases, however, and their shape turns horizontal. In contrast to the oldest Turkish children in this study, the oldest German children do not succeed in drawing the house significantly often in perspective.

Statistical Evaluation of the Results

Remarks on the Presentation of the Results

The phantom drawings have provided a visual presentation of the results that has many advantages over numerical tables. However, there is one shortcoming to this visual presentation: while differences in configurations are easily perceived, the statistical significance of these differences cannot be interpreted with certainty. The results of the following two studies, produced using analysis of variance and the technique of loglinear models, should help to compensate for this shortcoming. In fact, the results of these studies, one on the building size and the other on additional architectural variables, should be used as additional captions to the phantom drawings. The first of the studies treats one of the most important architectural variables: the relative size of buildings and windows. In the second study the technique of loglinear models is applied to other distinctive building features in order to pinpoint the influences exerted on these by the parameters of age (A), building type (B), and culture (C), or their interactions. In addition to the first two studies concerning architectural features, there are two more studies complementing the phantom drawings with data on nonarchitectural features (e.g., human figures, plants, etc.) and on typical developmental features (e.g., scribbles, transparencies, etc.), which cannot be shown in phantom drawings.

Relative Sizes of Buildings and Windows

Building Size

The relative sizes of the six building types for Turkish and German children can be seen in Table 9.8.

The Friedman two-way analysis of variance applied to these data shows that the size of the building shape turns out to be a significant source of variance as Turkish and German children grow older. This confirms the suggestion proposed in the interpretation of the phantom drawings that nondimensional size (huge vs. tiny) used first as a distinctive feature is later replaced by dimensional size. As can be seen from Table 9.8, the apartment building remains among the largest in size throughout the three age groups for Turkish and German children alike.

Window Size

The relative sizes of the windows of the six building types for Turkish and German children is shown in Table 9.9.

Again, the Friedman two-way analysis of variance shows that window size becomes an increasing source of variance for the buildings as the Turkish and German children grow older. From Table 9.9 it can be seen that the office and school remain among the buildings with the largest windows for all three age groups of both Turkish and German children.

Table 9.8. Difference between the Mean Size Ranks of Six Building Types
for Three Age Groups of Two Nationalities

Age and nationality	Difference in mean size ranks[a]						p (chi-square)
	O	F	R	S	A	H	
3–5 years of age							
Turkish	3.71	4.00	3.00	4.29	4.14	1.86	0.128
German	4.57	3.86	2.79	3.57	4.14	2.07	0.131
6–7 years of age							
Turkish	2.96	3.99	2.86	4.21	4.57	2.42	0.000
German	3.83	3.68	3.43	4.55	3.80	1.70	0.000
8–12 years of age							
Turkish	4.40	2.20	3.75	3.45	4.85	2.35	0.006
German	2.91	3.22	3.47	4.38	4.97	2.06	0.000

[a]O, office building; F, factory; R, religious building (mosque or church); S, school; A, apartment building; H, house.

Table 9.9. Difference between the Mean Size Ranks of the Windows in Six
Building Types for Three Age Groups of Two Nationalities

Age and nationality	Difference in mean size ranks						p (chi-square)
	O	F	R	S	A	H	
3–5 years of age							
Turkish	3.36	3.86	3.14	4.71	4.14	1.79	0.070
German	2.93	4.29	2.57	4.07	4.36	2.79	0.240
6–7 years of age							
Turkish	3.07	3.61	3.13	4.07	3.77	3.36	0.079
German	2.90	3.07	3.24	4.31	3.95	3.53	0.032
8–12 years of age							
Turkish	4.90	1.85	3.35	3.15	4.25	3.50	0.009
German	4.93	2.70	3.53	3.40	2.63	3.80	0.010

Note. See Table 9.8 for explanation of abbreviations.

The Correlation between Building Size and Window Size

That the size of a window in a drawing of a building would depend on the size of the building shape seems logical: the larger the building shape, the larger the windows, and vice versa. The assumption that there would be significant correlations between building size and window size was born out for all Turkish age groups and for all German age groups except the oldest one. The results can be studied in Table 9.10.

Table 9.10. Correlations between Building Size and Window Size
for Turkish and German Children

Age groups	Correlations			
	Turkish children		German children	
	rho	tau	rho	tau
3–5 years	.698	.579	.320	.243
	$p = .001$	$p = .001$	$p = .039$	$p = .041$
6–7 years	.456	.346	.297	.228
	$p = .001$	$p = .001$	$p = .001$	$p = .001$
8–12 years	.622	.517	.100	.075
	$p = .001$	$p = .001$	$p = .334$	$p = .342$

Other Architectural Variables

Variables Studied

In addition to the size of buildings and windows, the other variables used in the construction of the phantom drawings were studied using the technique of loglinear models. These variables were:

- External building shape: verticality/horizontality, presence of secondary building, and form of the roof.
- Internal facade structure: number of stories, number of windows, and verticality of windows.

The results of the statistical investigation on the three possible sources of influence on these architectural features—age (A), building type (B), and culture (C), and their interactions—are presented variable by variable in the following pages.

Verticality/Horizontality. The question of verticality/horizontality of these building types was investigated with the parameters AX, BX, CX, and ACX. It was found that the verticality/horizontality of a building drawing depended, on the one hand, on the age of the children and, on the other hand, on the building type (AX: p = .01; BX: p = .01; fit of the model, p = .59). Children aged 3–7 years drew vertical buildings very frequently. The number of horizontal buildings increased in the 8- to 12-year-old age group. The apartment building and office were the most vertical, while the factory and church were the most horizontal. The school and house varied strongly in their proportions. While the factory belonged to the horizontal buildings, there was a definite cultural influence: Turkish children drew the factory as the most horizontal building less frequently than did their German peers. This outcome might have been influenced by the fact that the only factory in the city of Trabzon that could have served as the model for some of the drawings was vertical in shape.

Secondary Buildings. The question of the presence/absence of a secondary building (smokestack or steeple) was investigated again with the model parameters AX, BX, CX, and ACX. It was found that whether or not a secondary building was present in a drawing depended on the age of the children but more strongly on the building type. Culture, too, played a significant role (AX: p = .01; BX: p = .001; CX: p = .01; fit of the model, p = .57).

With increasing age, the children tended to draw more secondary buildings. But these occurred only in connection with the factory (smokestack) and religious building (minaret or steeple). The cultural influence can be seen in the fact that the German children drew secondary buildings more frequently than did the Turkish.

Form of the Roof. This variable was studied with the model parameters AX, ACX, BCX. It was found that variety of roof forms drawn depended on the age of the children but more strongly on the building type; it depended also on an interaction between building type and culture (AX: p = .05; BX: p = .001; BCX: p = .05; fit of the model, p = .41). With increasing age, children produced a larger variety of roof forms. But the office, factory, and apartment building were mostly shown with flat roofs. Tne house, in contrast, was very seldom drawn with a flat roof. The fact that Turkish children drew the office more often with a flat roof than their German peers mut be considered a regional (cultural) influence.

The form of the roof was especially studied for the two kinds of religious buildings (mosque and church) using the parameters AX, CX, and ACX. As was expected, the form of the roof on the religious buildings depended strongly on culture (CX: p = .001; fit of the model, p = .14). Turkish children drew the mosque very often with a dome, whereas the dome never occurred in the German children's drawings of the church and only once in a drawing of another building. This result clearly shows the influence of the environment on children's drawings of building types as they grow older. I would venture the hypothesis that the difference in the presence of domes found between Turkish and German children would be paralleled between Italian and German children since domes can be frequently found in Italian church buildings.

Number of Stories. The number of stories was investigated by employing the parameters AX, ACX, and BCX. It was found that there was some increase in the number of stories drawn reflecting an increase in age, but the strongest influence determining the number of stories was the building type; in addition, culture tended to play a role in how many stories were drawn (AX: p = .05; BX: p = .001; CX: p = .05; fit of the model, p = .30). While children tended to draw their buildings with more stories as they grew older, factories, religious buildings, and houses had few stories in the drawings—most one or two. In contrast, the apartment building had many stories. The office and school had the greatest variation in the number of stories attributed to them. On the whole, the buildings of the Turkish children were drawn with less stories than the buildings of their German peers. This must be regarded as a cultural influence. For example, in the drawings by the Turkish children, the school was often a building with one or two stories only, while the German children frequently drew the school with more than two stories. Even the house often had more than two stories.

Number of Windows. This variable was investigated by employing the parameters AX, ACX, and BCX. The number of windows drawn was strongly influenced by the age of the children, the building type, and the culture (AX: $p =$ .001; BX: $p = .001$; CX: $p = .001$; fit of the model, $p = .30$). With increasing age, children drew more windows. But only the apartment building had a large number of windows. The office and school varied strongly in the number of windows allotted to them. The factory, church, and house were always drawn with few windows. On the whole, Turkish children drew less windows than their German peers. The apartment building and school in particular tended to have more windows in the drawings of the German children than in those of the Turkish children.

Does the Office Have the Largest Windows? The relative size of the buildings' windows was studied, as reported above, by analysis of variance, because relative size data stemmed from the rank order of window size for the six building types. While data with an ordinal level of measure should not be analyzed using the technique of loglinear models, the question of whether one of the six buildings had larger windows than the rest can be studied in this way. It was investigated for the office building, employing AX a a model parameter. The office was in fact often drawn with the largest windows as children grew older (AX: $p = .01$; fit of the model, $p = .45$).

Verticality/Horizontality of Windows. The proportions of windows was studied using BX and ACX as model parameters. It was found that the proportions of windows depended on the age of the children, the building, the culture, and the interaction of age and culture (AX: $p = .001$; BX: $p = .01$; CX: $p =$ .001; ACX: $p = .001$; fit of the model, $p = .53$).

The older the children grew, the less vertical and the more horizontal the windows became. In the end it was only the religious buildings that tended to have vertical windows. German children, however, drew more vertical windows than the Turkish. The older Turkish children (8–12 years) drew an exceptional amount of horizontal windows. The reason for this discrepancy must cultural.

Nonarchitectural Variables (Y) in the Drawings

Window Adornment

Whether windows were embellished by curtains, crossbars, or other decorations has been studied using the model parameters AY, BY, and CY. It was found that window adornment depended heavily on age and culture and, to a lesser albeit significant extent, on the building type (AY: $p = .001$; BY: $p = .05$; CY:

$p = .001$; fit of the model, $p = .77$). Window decoration developed with the age of the children. It was very frequent in the windows of the office building and the house. German children drew more window decorations than their Turkish counterparts. This must be regarded as a cultural influence.

Elaboration of the Roof

Elaboration of the roof (with tiles or hatching) was investigated with the model parameters AY, BY, CY, and ACY. The result was that elaboration of the roof depended significantly on the nationality of the children (CY: $p = .01$; fit of the model, $p = .01$). German children elaborated the roof of their buildings significantly more often than did their Turkish peers—a fact that can only be accounted for by cultural difference. There was a general tendency also for roof elaboration to increase with age.

Addition of Chimneys

Whether the children drew chimneys and on which buildings they placed them was investigated using the model parameters ACY and BCY. It emerged that the presence of chimneys depended strongly on the building type and on the interaction of building type and culture (BY: $p = .001$; BCY: $p = .01$; fit of the model, $p = .37$). Chimneys were very frequently drawn on factories, and very seldom on religious buildings and schools. However, the German children drew more chimneys on schools and office buildings than the Turkish children. This must be a cultural effect.

Smoke from Chimneys

Children drew chimneys with or without smoke. Were there any particular influences favoring the drawing of smoke? This question was studied with the parameters ACY and BCY. It was found that the building type was the main influence on whether smoke was drawn, but culture also played a role (BY: $p = .001$; BCY: $p = .05$; fit of the model, $p = .69$). Smoke was drawn very frequently with the factory but almost never with the religious building. German children drew smoke more frequently on the chimneys of office buildings and schools than did the Turkish children (who seldom drew chimneys on these buildings). But Turkish children drew smoke on factories more often than did the German children. Both facts must be influenced by differences in culture.

Drawings of Elements in the Surroundings of a Building

Children did not only draw the buildings, but frequently added pathways leading up to them or added plants or trees indicating a garden. The question of whether any special factor influenced the occurrence of elements in the surroundings of the building was investigated by using BY, CY, and ACY as model parameters. It was found that building and cultural factors played a role in the drawing of elements in the surroundings of a building (BY: $p = .01$; CY: $p = .001$; fit of the model, $p = .99$). In fact, it was in the surroundings of houses that elements were more often added, and these additions were seldom in the surroundings of the religious or apartment buildings. Turkish children drew elements in the surroundings of their buildings more often than did German children. This result was confirmed in a study using CY and ACY as parameters. In this study, only culture turned out to be a significant parameter (CY: $p = .001$; fit of the model, $p = .50$). Turkish children clearly drew buildings with elements in their surroundings more often than did German children.

Addition of Human Figures

Sometimes children added human figures to their drawings. Which factors influenced the drawing of human figures was studied by using AY, BY, CY, and ACY as model parameters. The result was that age, building type, and nationality played a role in influencing the drawing of human figures (AY: $p = .001$; BY: $p = .01$; CY: $p = .001$; fit of the model, $p = .98$). Human figures were drawn most frequently by the 6- and 7-year-olds and very seldom in the group of 8- to 12-year-olds. They occurred most frequently in the context of the office and factory. Turkish children drew more human figures than did their German peers. This must again be considered a cultural difference.

Developmental Variables (Z)

Variables Studied

Some of the main developmental variables that apply to drawings of buildings as well as to drawings of other subject matter have been condensed into the global rating scores. The results of the study conducted with the global rating scores have been reported above. They showed that the main parameter in the loglinear model of drawing development is age.

In this study on specific developmental variables in children's drawings, scribbles, transparencies, attempts to draw perspective, complex roof forms (as indicators of pseudo-perspectives or perspectives), and the presence of doors in the buildings (as indicators of a more advanced stage of development) have been studied separately.

Scribbles

Whether a child drew scribbles, which are an indicator of the sensorimotor stage of intelligence, was studied with the children aged 3–6 years by applying the model parameters AZ and ACZ. It was found that the presence of scribbles in the drawings depended exclusively on age (AZ: $p = .001$; fit of the model, $p = .39$). The younger the children, the more scribbles they drew. This was true regardless of the nationality and, hence, was independent of culture.

Transparencies and Interiors

Transparencies as an indicator, applied in particular to the phase of intellectual realism, were studied using AZ and ACZ as parameters. Transparencies were found to depend clearly on age (AZ: $p = .01$; fit of the model, $p = .46$). Transparencies were drawn significantly more often in the 6- to 7-year-old age group than in either the youngest or oldest groups and did not depend on nationality (i.e., culture).

We also asked which model parameters influenced the drawing of interiors, be it as part of a transparency, a look through a window, or without any features of the building exterior. This question was answered by applying the parameters AZ, BZ, and ACZ. It was found that interior drawings were connected to age but mainly to building type (AZ: $p = .05$; BZ: $p = .001$; fit of the model, $p = .94$). Interior drawings occurred mostly in the 6- to 7-year-old age group, and they were more frequent in the office than in any other building type and least frequent in the house. As has been suggested above, children may not be familiar with offices as building types, but rather, in terms of the activities happening within them.

Different Building Views

The question of whether the buildings were drawn from the front, from a combination of front and side views, or whether an attempt was made at perspective was investigated with the parameters AZ and CZ. The result was that perspective depended significantly on age (AZ: $p = .05$; fit of the model, $p = .052$). Drawings employed side views only decreased with age. Drawings combining front and side views and attempts to draw a perspective increased equally with age. Pseudo-perspectives were most frequent in the children aged 6–7 years.

When BZ was introduced as a parameter together with ACZ to investigate the development of different building views, it was found that the building type influenced the building view (BZ: $p = .01$; fit of the model, $p = .85$). Flat side views were especially frequent with the factory and the religious building, whereas the house was most frequently drawn in pseudo-perspective or in perspective.

The range of views including perspective increased significantly with age, as was found for Turkish (H test, $p = .05$) and German children (H test, $p = .01$).

Complexity of Roof Form

The roof might be drawn flat, peaked, in a saddle form, or in the most complex form—a combination of a triangular peak with a saddle roof. The question of whether the occurrence of this most complex form was dependent on some parameter was investigated by employing ACZ as a parameter. The occurrence of the most complex roof form was significantly dependent on age (AZ: $p = .05$; fit of the model, $p = 1.00$). The number of complex roof forms increased with age. But the range of different roof forms increased with age more for Turkish children than for German children (H test, $p = .001$, for Turkish children, not significant for German children).

Presence of a Door

At first glance, a door would seem to be an architectural variable. In this study, however, it turned out to be a developmental variable. When the presence of doors in the building drawings was investigated with AZ and ACZ as parameters, age turned out to be a highly significant influence (AZ: $p = .001$; fit of the model, $p = .94$). Doors were least often drawn by children aged 3–5 years. By the ages of 8 to 12 years, they were drawn almost always on all building types.

Religious Symbols

The question of whether religious symbols were drawn with the mosque and church was investigated by employing ACZ as a parameter. It was found that the frequency of the presence of a crescent or a cross on a religious building was a matter of age and culture (AZ: $p = .001$; CZ: $p = .01$; fit of the model, $p = 1.00$). The older the children were, the more frequently they drew religious symbols on religious buildings. Religious symbols occurred more frequently, however, on churches than on mosques.

Summary of Significant Cultural Differences

The phantom drawings and the results of the studies using the technique of loglinear models can be summarized by three tables of distinctive architectural features. Each table refers to a different age group and contains the results, listed separately for Turkish and German children, in terms of plus and minus signs signaling whether, on the average, a feature in a drawing was more prevalent or less prevalent or tended to be large or small (Tables 9.11-9.13).

If the plus or minus sign is different for Turkish and German children a difference between their drawings with respect to a particular distinctive feature has been found in the studies. Such a difference must be attributed to culture. In children aged 3–5 years, 11 such differences were discovered, most of them for the drawings of the school (5) and the apartment building (3). The largest number of differences (16) between Turkish and German children was noted for the 6- to 7-year-olds, most of them in the drawings of offices (5), factories (4), and schools (3). The 8- to 12-year-old Turkish and German children differed on the

Table 9.11. Distinctive Architectural Features of Six Building Types for Turkish and German Children Aged 3–5 Years

	Presence or absence of feature[a]											
	O		F		R		S		A		H	
Distinctive features	T	G	T	G	T	G	T	G	T	G	T	G
Size	−	+	+	+	−	−	+	−	+	+	−	−
Verticality	+	+	−	−	+	+	−	+	−	+	+	+
Sec. building	−	−	−	−	−	−	−	−	−	−	−	−
Roof	−	−	−	−	−	+	−	+	−	−	+	+
Stories	+	+	−	−	−	−	−	+	−	+	−	−
No. of windows	+	+	−	+	−	−	+	+	+	+	−	−
Size of windows	−	−	+	+	−	−	+	+	+	+	−	−
Vertic. of windows	−	−	−	−	+	+	−	+	−	+	−	−

[a]O, office building; F, factory; R, religious building (mosque or church); S, school; A, apartment building; H, house; T, Turkish children; G, German children.

Table 9.12. Distinctive Architectural Features of Six Building Types for Turkish and German Children Aged 6–7 Years

	Presence or absence of feature											
	O		F		R		S		A		H	
Distinctive features	T	G	T	G	T	G	T	G	T	G	T	G
Size	−	+	+	−	−	−	+	+	+	+	−	−
Verticality	+	+	+	−	+	−	−	+	+	+	−	+
Sec. building	−	−	(+)	+	(+)	+	−	−	−	−	−	−
Roof	−	+	−	−	+	+	+	+	−	−	+	+
Stories	−	+	−	−	−	−	−	−	+	+	−	−
No. of windows	−	+	−	+	−	−	−	+	+	+	−	−
Size of windows	−	−	+	−	−	−	+	+	+	+	−	+
Vertic. of windows	−	+	−	−	+	+	−	+	−	+	−	−

Note. See Table 9.11 for explanation of abbreviations. Pluses in parentheses indicate occurring tendencies.

smallest number (10) of distinctive features, mostly for the office (4) and the school (3). This means that the difference between Turkish and German children in the use of distinctive architectural features is most pronounced during the phase of intellectual realism, when they "draw what they know." This result is also confirmed by its converse—the buildings drawn with all eight distinctive architectural features looking alike. This is the case for the house in the youngest group, for the factory and the house in the oldest. The 6- to 7-year-old Turkish

Table 9.13. Distinctive Architectural Features of Six Building Types for Turkish and German Children Aged 8–12 Years

	Presence or absence of feature											
	O		F		R		S		A		H	
Distinctive features	T	G	T	G	T	G	T	G	T	G	T	G
Size	+	−	−	−	+	+	−	+	+	+	−	−
Verticality	+	−	−	−	−	−	+	−	+	+	−	−
Sec. building	−	−	+	+	+	+	−	−	−	−	−	−
Roof	−	+	−	−	+	+	+	+	−	+	+	+
Stories	+	−	−	−	−	−	+	−	+	+	−	−
No. of windows	+	+	+	+	−	−	+	+	+	+	−	−
Size of windows	+	+	−	−	−	+	−	−	+	−	+	+
Vertic. of windows	−	−	−	−	+	+	−	−	−	−	−	−

Note. See Table 9.11 for explanation of abbreviations.

and German children did not draw any of the six building types with exactly the same distinctive features.

If the different building types are compared with respect to the distinctive features listed in the tables, the factory, religious building, apartment house, and house are easily distinguished by oppositions of their features. In contrast, the office and apartment building or school are more difficult to distinguish in some cases. For the oldest Turkish children, for example, there is no difference between the features of office and apartment building. And for the oldest German children the features of office and school are fairly alike. For both older Turkish and German children there are only two or three features opposing office and school. This lack of distinctiveness in the drawings of offices derives probably from both a lack of an architectural stereotype and the fact that the office is best known for the activities going on inside of it. On the other hand, there is a confusion of functions factually occurring in both cultural situations. The offices in a smaller Turkish city are very often located in buildings otherwise being used as apartment houses. And offices in smaller German cities are often located in the house of the owner. The fact that school buildings might get confused with office buildings is unfortunately true for many situations. Perhaps it is for that reason that Turkish children used the flag as the main distinctive feature for the school. In any event, the results of these studies show that cross-culturally there are some very distinctive building types (factory, religious building, apartment building, and house), whereas other building types tend to be less distinctive within a culture, and distinctive to a varying degree between cultures (office, school). This lack of distinctiveness could be used as an index of poor environmental quality because, according to the model developed at the beginning of this book, distinctiveness must be rooted in the built environment.

The significant differences in distinctive architectural features resulting from variations in the cultural environment of the children, as indicated using the technique of loglinear models, can now be summarized:

- Turkish children drew less horizontal factories than their German counterparts.
- German children drew secondary buildings (smokestacks, steeples) more frequently than did Turkish children.
- Turkish children drew the office with a flat roof more often than the German children.
- Turkish children drew the religious building with a dome more often than the German children. In fact, the latter never used a dome on their religious building, and a dome was found only once in all their drawings.

- Turkish children drew fewer stories in their buildings than did the German children, particularly in the case of the school and the house.
- Turkish children drew fewer windows in their buildings than German children, especially in the drawings of the school and the apartment building.
- German children drew more vertical windows than the Turkish children. The 8- to 12-year-old Turkish children in particular drew many horizontal windows.

It is plausible that most of these differences are rooted in the built environment of the children. A case in point is the dome in the religious building of the Turkish children.

But further cultural differences were also found for nonarchitectural variables. These, too, may ultimately be a result of environmental differences:

- German children drew more window adornments and elaborate roofs than their Turkish peers.
- German children drew chimneys on offices and schools more often than the Turkish.
- Chimneys issued smoke more often in the German drawings.
- The factories in the drawings of Turkish children had smoke issuing from smokestacks more often than the factories in the drawings of the German children.
- Turkish children drew more surrounding elements (plants, trees, pathways, etc.) and human figures than did the Germans.

As was expected, there were no particular developmental variables with cultural differences. It was only found that Turkish children as they grew older drew more complex roof forms than the Germans. Also, the German children used more religious symbols on their drawings of churches than Turkish children on their mosques. But the latter difference might also stem from the environment.

On the whole, it has been shown that the null hypothesis maintaining equal use of distinctive architectural features in the drawings of building types made by children from two different cultures must in many instances be rejected.

Discussion of the Results

Accomplishments and Shortcomings

In the last part of this book I will balance the accomplishments of the central study against those shortcomings which could provoke criticism. What has been accomplished can be established by confronting the results of the central study with the four hypotheses spelled out earlier.

As far as the first hypothesis is concerned, it has not been possible to detect any crucial differences in the global drawing development between the children from two fairly different cultures—Turkish and German. The typical stages of development—scribbling, fortuitous and failed realism (or incapacity to synthesize), intellectual realism, and visual realism—observed initially in French and Swiss children by Luquet (1927) and Piaget and Inhelder (1948/1967) have been shown to hold for German and Turkish children alike.

With regard to the second hypothesis, similar results were found when studying the development of grapheme systems, which, according to Olivier (1974), should furnish the building blocks of children's drawings. Turkish and German children develop the same graphemes in the same sequence as did Olivier's French children. On the basis of these results, it is plausible to conclude that children's drawings depend in their form to a large extent on the maturation of inborn muscular and perceptual abilities.

This conclusion is confirmed if we turn to the test of the third hypothesis concerning grapheme development in physically disabled and normal children within one culture. These two groups of German children proved significantly different in their ability to draw the symmetrical graphemes of system G3, although they were alike on the earlier grapheme systems G1 and G2. Ability to draw, according to the tests of the first three hypotheses, is therefore, more a matter of ''nature'' than of ''nurture.''

Culture enters the picture, however, if the distinctive architectural features with which Turkish and German children distinguish different building types are compared. The fourth alternative hypothesis stated that in order to differentiate between building types, children would use variations of distinctive architectural features. In this study the crucial features were relative size, verticality/horizontality, form of roof, presence or absence of secondary buildings to designate the building shape; and number of stories and windows, relative size of windows, and verticality/horizontality of windows to define the facade structure of different building types. The fourth alternative hypothesis was confirmed for many of these features, at least for the older children. Therefore, it appears that drawings are used by the children for representing to themselves and to others features present in the environment of their material culture.

Compared to these clear-cut results, the role played by drawing ability in the present investigation could still give occasion for criticism. Granted that drawing ability was shown to develop in the same way in Turkish and German children, was the assessment of children's architectural concepts really best accomplished using drawings? Would not the children's lack of drawing skill interfere with expressing the images present in their minds? Would their skill in drawing correspond to their ability to recognize a building or would ''simple recognition run ahead of drawing''? This was the case in the visual recognition of cutout shapes first perceived only by touch in the Piaget and Inhelder experiment (1948/1967) that I reported at the beginning of this book. This was also the contention of Freeman (1980), which I dealt with briefly: ''The child knows more than he draws.'' This first potential criticism will be dealt with in this discussion by means of two control studies designed to shed light on the problem of drawing versus recognition.

The second potential criticism that has to be dealt with evolves around the notion of context. There is a growing conviction among students of semiotics that signs are not understood by themselves but in the context of other signs and their use. Thus recognition of building types taken as architectural signs would be possible only in an urban context. The isolation of single building types as prescribed by the task given to the children in this study would be deemed artificial and not representative of the recognition situation in the field. This second potential criticism will be considered in the final part of the discussion.

Further Evidence from Two Control Studies on Children's Recognition of Building Types from Pictures

Control Study 1: Free Sorting of Building Pictures

The Problem of the First Control Study

The first control study was designed to investigate children's ability to differentiate buildings without recurring to drawing ability. The study tries to answer the question of whether children could better imagine different building types when recognizing pictures than when asked to draw them.

Recognition Test versus Reproduction Test

There is evidence in the psychological literature on learning in favor of the argument that it is easier to recognize learning material than to reproduce it (Osgood, 1958). Piaget had repeatedly found that "simple recognition (was) running ahead of drawing" (Piaget & Inhelder, 1948/1967), although he did not attach any particular significance to this fact. Since the aim of this book is to clarify the role of children's drawings as iconic representations of their environment, an answer must be provided to the question of whether this representation of objects is delayed with respect to the simple recognition of objects.

Unobtrusive Free Sorting Tasks

The task the children were given in the main study of this book was to draw six building types. This task is clearly restrictive and leaves little room for personal expression. In contrast, in the control study on the recognition of buildings without employing graphic skills, the task was designed to be as unobtrusive as possible.

One way of conducting unobtrusive studies is to present the subjects with verbal or pictorial stimuli, and to limit impositions when giving them the task of sorting this material into any number of groups according to any criteria they choose. This free sorting technique had originally been applied by Miller (1969) to a sample of words drawn from a dictionary and printed on small cards. After his subjects had sorted these words according to their own criteria, the data were processed by the method of hierarchical cluster analysis (Johnson, 1967). This method proceeds from a diagonal item-by-item matrix in which at each intersection of two items, a/b, a/c, a/d, . . . a/x, a frequency is listed. This frequency corresponds to the number of subjects who have paired the two intersecting items in one of their freely sorted groupings. It is intuitively easy to understand that any two items in such a study could be placed by the subjects in any one of their groupings never, seldom, often, or always. The hierarchical cluster analysis provides dendrograms (treelike graphs) in which the items placed together by all or many of the subjects form the uppermost branches of the tree. The lowest branches springing from its stem separate all those groups of items that have, on the whole, never or seldom been sorted together. This is illustrated in Figure 10.1.

There are two strategies for constructing the trees, depending on the maximum or minimum "distances" between items in two clusters (branches) being selected as criteria for their fusion on the next lower hierarchical level. In practice, the "maximum solution" best fulfils the purpose of studies like the ones discussed here.

Miller (1969) found that the branches of the hierarchical tree resulted from the subjects sorting together clustered words of similar meaning, for example, words for humans, living things, objects, feelings, and other subject matter.

I have applied the free sorting technique to many kinds of materials, including a collection of buttons for operating electrical equipment, cigarette packs, pictures of women, women's hair styles, posters, furniture, etc. In addition to following Miller's technique, I used an "objective" method for interpreting the resulting hierarchical dendrograms: After the subjects had finished their sorting, they were asked to name their personal criteria for each of the groupings they had brought together. Thus, for each item, all the criteria were obtained that the subjects in the sample had attached to it. This provided a control for the in-

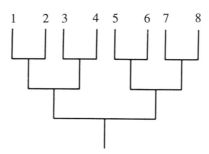

Figure 10.1. Schematic dendrogram resulting from hierarchical cluster analysis.

terpretation of each cluster in the dendrogram. Miller interpreted his clusters by referring to the impressionistic evidence gathered from looking at the items in them. But if the common denominator of the criteria attached to the items in a given cluster is used, a more "objective" interpretation is possible.

The division into clusters of items belonging to a common domain (like buttons, cigarette packs, women's pictures, etc.) reveals, semiotically speaking, the meaning these items have for the subjects who sorted them. Presumably they sorted items that appeared similar to them into common groups. Hence, meaning could be defined as "item similarity," and the common denominator of the criteria attached to the items in a cluster is an operationalization of meaning.

This method should also apply to pictures representing buildings of different functional meaning, if they were sorted and the sortings were commented upon. In our case, children would be given pictures of different office buildings, factories, religious buildings, schools, apartment building, and houses. They would be asked to sort them, putting similar pictures together into a common pile. After having finished their sorting, they would be asked to name the criteria which had prompted them to put certain building pictures together in the piles.

If the pictures are given to children of different age groups, we would expect the dendrograms for the younger children to be more diffuse, whereas the older children should, ideally, end up with a dendrogram of six clusters, one for each of the six building types. But different age groups are not even needed. The objective of this control study is to compare simple recognition with the drawings of different building types. Since drawing ability increases with age, it would be sufficient to compare only two younger age groups. By giving nursery school children the task of sorting building pictures, it could be established whether they were able to recognize the functional meaning of some of the six building types. By asking them the name of the buildings in a cluster, it would be easy to find out which building types these are.

If the nursery school children of this control study were able to identify more building types by recognition than their peers in the main study were able to draw, we would be forced to conclude that drawings were not the best way to access children's mental images.

Hypothesis of the First Control Study

What is expected in terms of results from this control study can now be expressed in terms of a null hypothesis and its alternatives. The null hypothesis could be phrased as follows:

There is no difference in the mental image of the six building types in nursery school children. They do not recognize the functional meaning of appropriately drawn building pictures if they sort them according to similarity. The dendrogram resulting from their free sortings is completely diffuse.

If the null hypotheses is rejected by empirical evidence, an alternative hypothesis might be:

Nursery school children differentiate between some but not all building types when sorting pictures of buildings. For instance, they will confuse the office and apartment building. The dendrogram resulting from their free sortings of building pictures will be simply but clearly structured.

Method of the Free Sorting Study

The Building Pictures. The building pictures used in this study were drawn on 10×10 cm tracing paper and copied using heliographic print. Each resulting copy was numbered on the back. The 30 building pictures are given in Figures 10.2–10.7.

Figure 10.2 represents five office buildings that are large and vertical in shape with many uniform windows, window bands, or curtain walls on six stories. Figure 10.3 shows five large and vertical four- or six-story apartment buildings, each of which is distinguished from the office buildings by the addition of balconies and a variety of window sizes. Figure 10.4 shows five pictures of churches, which are mainly marked by steeples. The five factories in Figure 10.5 are distinguished by smokestacks, shed roofs, or window bands. Figure 10.6 presents five pictures of single- or two-story houses with few windows. Figure 10.7 shows five school buildings. Like the houses, they are two stories, but they are larger than the houses and feature larger windows.

Children's Groups. The 50 children who participated in this study were contacted in five different nursery schools in southern Germany—four in different parts of Schwäbisch Gmünd and its surroundings (Schwäbisch Gmünd–West, Saint Mary, Spreitbach) and one in Ravensburg. The age of the children ranged between 4 to 6 years. Their average age was 5.14 years.

Procedure. The data were collected in the rooms of the different nursery schools. A well-shuffled deck of approximately playing-card size with the 30 building pictures was handed to each child. The children were invited to play a game with these pictures and, after the game, to take them home and color them. They were to sort the cards into piles that had similar pictures in them, and they were allowed to make as many piles as they wanted. After the children had finished the sorting task, they were asked why they had placed each pile of

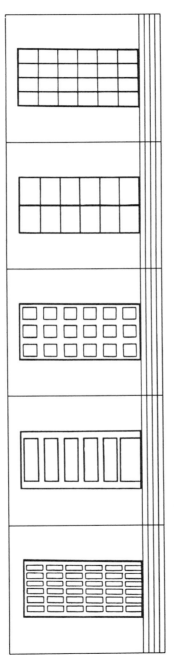

Figure 10.2. Five drawings of office buildings.

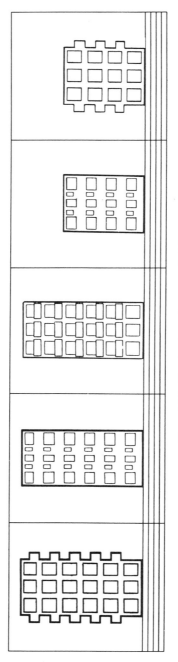

Figure 10.3. Five drawings of apartment buildings.

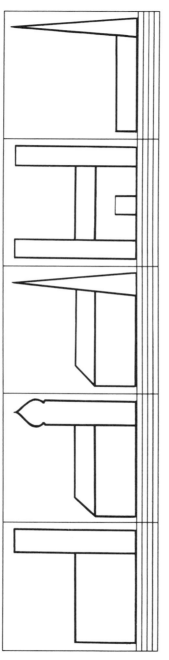

Figure 10.4. Five drawings of churches.

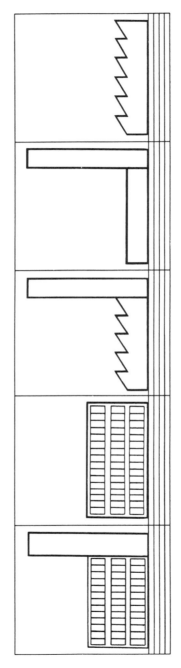

Figure 10.5. Five drawings of factories.

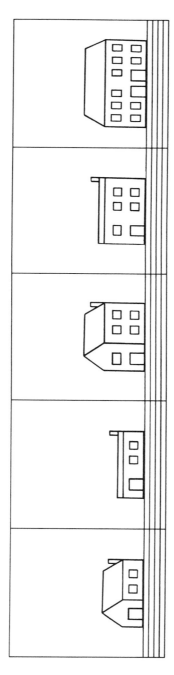

Figure 10.6. Five drawings of houses.

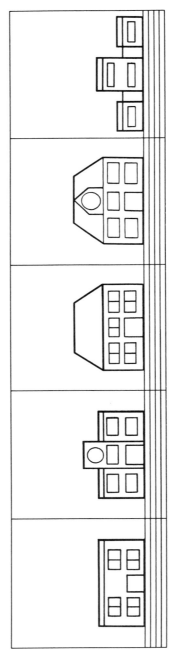

Figure 10.7. Five drawings of schools.

pictures together. The number of each picture in every pile and the reason for grouping the pictures together was then noted, and the card packs were given to the children after the procedure was terminated.

Analysis of the Data. In order to get some idea about the reliability of the procedure, the data were first split in two halves and processed separately according to the Johnson hierarchical cluster analysis (Johnson, 1967). The two resulting dendrograms were compared and found to be similar. Therefore, the data were pooled and processed together by the same program once more. The resulting dendrogram was then interpreted in terms of the pictures and the criteria for the groupings given by the children. The criteria for each building picture were derived by first inspecting for the pile in which a given picture had been placed, and then attaching the label given by the child to the whole pile. Since over 50 children participated in this study, each of the 30 building pictures had 50 criteria attached to it. In order to interpret a single cluster, the 50 criteria for each of the building pictures in that cluster were lumped together and inspected for the most frequently occurring label for all the pictures in that cluster.

Results of the First Control Study

Split-Half Comparison. The Johnson hierarchical cluster analysis yielded a (''maximum'') solution with three main clusters for each of the two halves of the data that had been processed separately. The two solutions are given separately in Figures 10.8 and 10.9.

A comparison between the three clusters contained in the first half and in the second half of the data shows that the clusters in both halves are identical. The data were, therefore, pooled and processed together.

The Dendrogram of the Pooled Data. The maximum solution for the pooled data once again yielded three clusters. This solution is given in Figure 10.10.

When the numbers in Figure 10.10 are substituted by their corresponding building pictures, the result is Figure 10.11.

From Figure 10.11 we can see that the first cluster consists exclusively of four- to six-story vertical buildings with many windows. The common denominator of the criteria given by the children for the building pictures in this cluster is clearly ''high-rise buildings'' (German: *Hochhäuser*).

The second cluster contains all buildings with a secondary building, smokestack, or steeple. But there are three subclusters to be observed. The first subcluster contains buildings with a parallel-sided, vertical secondary building. The criteria given by the children show that they did not always know what the

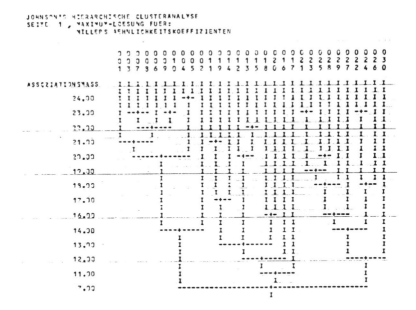

Figure 10.8. Maximum solution of the hierarchical cluster analysis for the first half of the data.

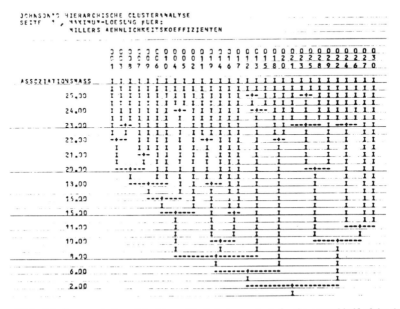

Figure 10.9. Maximum solution of the hierarchical cluster analysis for the second half of the data.

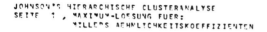

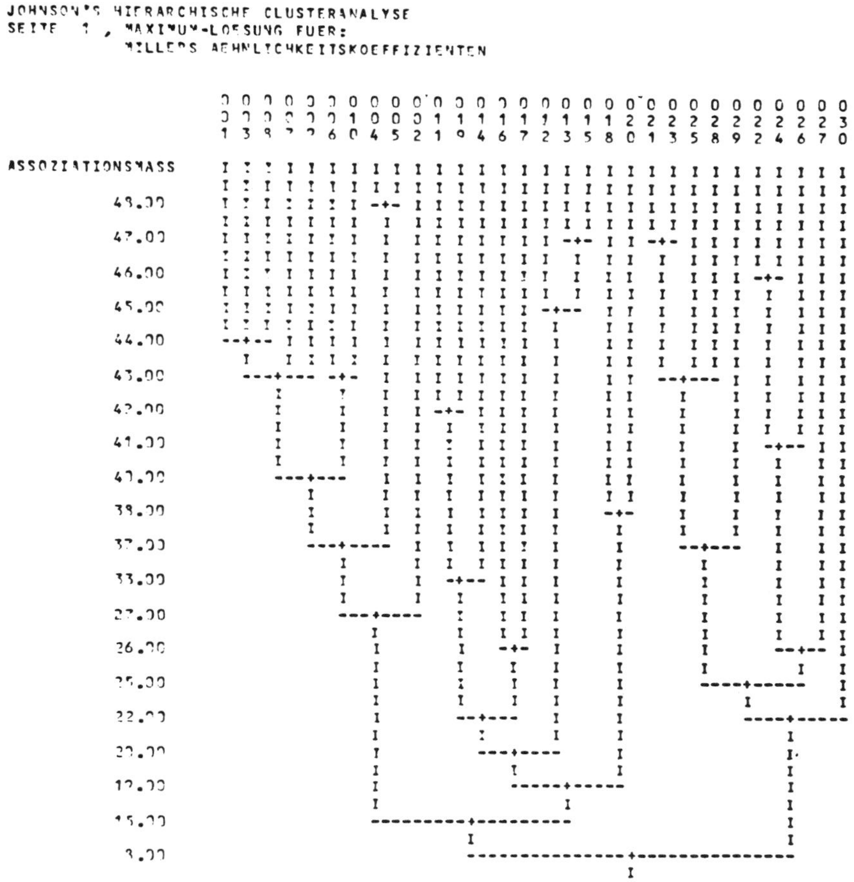

JOHNSON'S HIERARCHISCHE CLUSTERANALYSE
SEITE 1 , MAXIMUM-LOESUNG FUER:
MILLERS AEHNLICHKEITSKOEFFIZIENTEN

Figure 10.10. Maximum solution of the hierarchical cluster analysis for the pooled data.

pictures represented. But when they gave a name to a building, the designation "church" was most frequent, immediately followed by "factory." Another frequent label was "tower." But most comments were "don't know" or other descriptions like "flat roof" or "without a roof." According to the children's criteria, the second subcluster definitely contains churches. For the third subcluster, the largest category of comments is mixed ("don't know," "waves," "roofs," etc.), the second largest is "factory," followed by the smallest category "church."

The third cluster contains horizontal single- or two-story buildings with few

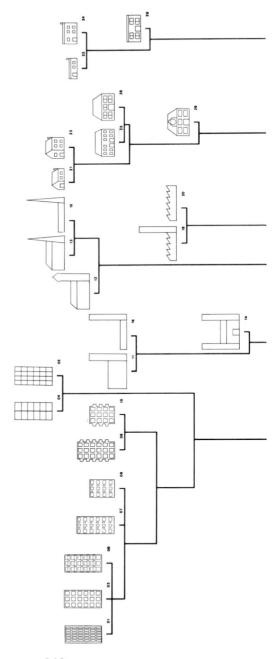

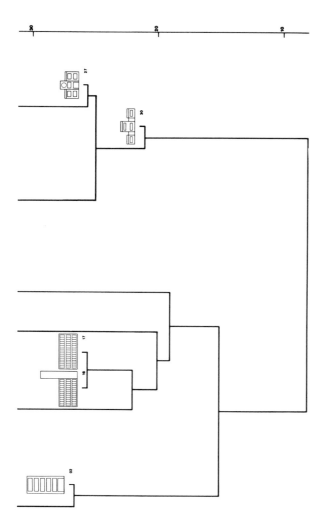

Figure 10.11. Maximum solution for the pooled data with building pictures substituted for numbers.

windows. There are two subclusters. The first contains buildings with saddle roofs, the second buildings with flat roofs. For the first subcluster, the label "(normal) house" predominates. In the second subcluster, the designation "(normal) house" still predominates, but there are other comments such as "don't know," "bungalow," "school," "office," or "factory" forming the second largest group of criteria, followed finally by the label "flat roof" or "flat building."

Discussion and Conclusion of This First Control Study

The null hypothesis that all buildings looked alike to the nursery school children must be rejected. There are three main building types the children recognized—high-rise buildings, buildings with secondary buildings attached (such as churches and factories), and "normal" houses.

Among the buildings accompanied by secondary buildings, the children distinguished between churches and factories. Office buildings and schools were apparently not distinguished and were very seldom given as sorting criteria. If these building functions were named at all, they seemed to be attached mostly to buildings in the third main cluster of low-story buildings with few windows.

This first control has shown that nursery school children are able to recognize different building types by reference to distinctive building features. On the other hand, their performance on the mere recognition task was not much different from the performance of their peers on the drawing task. Thus, the recognition task yielded only three instead of six clusters. Hence it does not appear to furnish better information than the drawing task as far as children's identification of building types is concerned. This is at least a good argument against the first potential criticism against drawings as an access to childrens' mental images that claims that direct recognition is a better approach to access children's images than drawings.

Control Study 2: Expressing the Mental Image of Building Types by Giving Building Pictures a Name

The Problem of the Second Control Study

The task of the second control study was to compare two methods of getting information on children's mental images of building types without recurring to the drawings they made of them.

Remember that the model of sign processes at the beginning of the book did not only provide a method of expressing mental images using drawings but also using words and even appropriate actions. The method of free sorting in the first control study yielded results that were not too different from those obtained by having children draw the building types. Therefore, the second control study was designed to render the recognition task even easier than in the first.

What could have been too difficult in the free sorting task? I sometimes found that adults, when asked to sort stimuli according to similarity, had difficulties in finding their own criteria for similarity. They usually asked which criteria to choose, and the answer was that they should define their own. In a sense, maybe, the free sorting task allows the subjects too much freedom. Therefore, in the second study the children were not even forced to find criteria for grouping the pictures. Hence, no grouping was requested and single pictures were responded to. If children were simply asked to tell what was represented on a building picture, it could be assumed that their recognition of the building type would prompt them to label it with the corresponding name.

Hypothesis of the Second Control Study

Consequently, the null hypothesis of the study was that there would be no difference between the results of the first and the second control studies.

An alternative hypothesis should then hold that children would distinguish better between building types in the second control study since their task was easier than in the first.

Method of the Simple Recognition Task

The Building Pictures. The building pictures in the second control study were the same as those that had been used in the study for the sorting task. This was expected to render the results of both studies comparable.

The Children. The 41 children participating in this study were contacted individually in private homes and nursery schools in Berlin and in Ulm (southern part of the FRG). Their ages ranged between 3:6 and 6:6 years, with an average of 5.24 years.

Procedure. Since data were collected either in private homes or in nursery schools, care had to be taken—especially in nursery schools—that children did not inform each other of the task. Each was told individually that children were taking part in a guessing game with picture cards and that they could keep the pictures after the game, take them home, and color them. The 30 pictures were then shown one by one in a random order. For each picture the question was asked: "What is on this picture?" The answers were noted on prepared coding sheets where each picture had a fixed number. As in the first control study, after the pictures had all been shown, the card pack was given to the child.

Analysis of the Data. The data for this type of study normally would be processed by content analysis. But in order to compare the two control studies, both had to be analyzed using the same method. Thus, the list of 30 answers from each child was transformed into a "pseudo-sorting" as follows: Answers in the second study were treated in the same way as the criteria for the piles of pictures that children had pronounced in the first study after having completed their sorting. For each child, pictures with identical answers were treated as pictures sorted together in one pile. The number of resulting piles was, of course, different for each child, depending on how many different answers had been given. But the result is comparable with the outcome of the first control study, where each child had his or her own number of piles with labels given to it—the only difference being that the labels had not been attached to the single pictures but to the piles after the sorting.

In this way the data of the second study can be processed like those in the first control study, using Johnson's hierarchical cluster analysis.

Finally, the dendrograms of the two control studies can be compared cluster by cluster to see whether they contain the same or different pictures. The similarity of the two partitions is calculated according to a criterion of Rand (1971), which may be found in textbooks on cluster analysis. If the index of the Rand criterion is high, the similarity between the partitions is high.

Results of the Second Control Study

The maximum solution of the Johnson hierarchical cluster analysis is shown in Figure 10.12.

As can be seen from Figure 10.12, there are four main clusters attached to the base of the dendrogram. The first contains ten pictures—all of buildings with a large vertical shape and many windows. These pictures had been called high-rise buildings by the majority of the children of this study.

The second cluster contains five pictures that had been labeled as churches by the majority (subclusters 37, 34, 32) or as churches by some and factories by others (subclusters 11, 19), the church label being more frequent than the factory label.

The third cluster contains eleven pictures that had been called houses by most of the children, with the exception of the pictures numbered 14 and 30 in Figure 10.11. Picture 14, which was not recognized by 9 of the 41 children, was

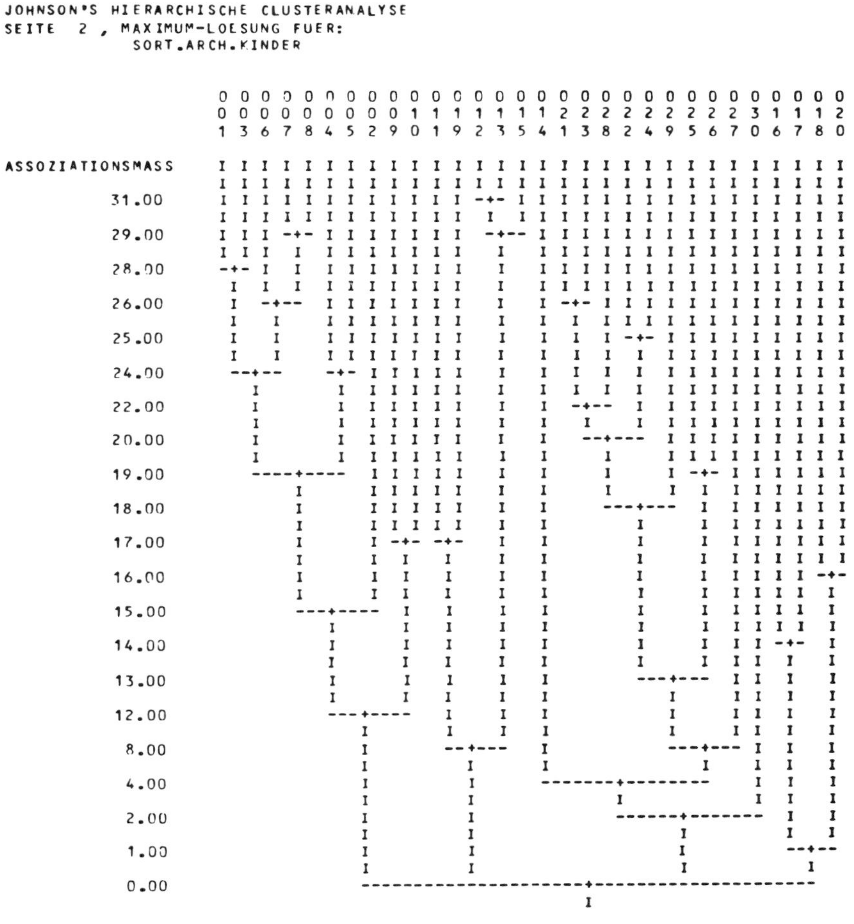

```
JOHNSON'S HIERARCHISCHE CLUSTERANALYSE
SEITE   2 , MAXIMUM-LOESUNG FUER:
        SORT.ARCH.KINDER

                        0 0 0 0 0 0 0 0 0 0 0 0 0 0 0 0 0 0 0 0 0 0 0 0 0 0 0 0 0 0
                        0 0 0 0 0 0 0 0 1 1 1 1 1 1 2 2 2 2 2 2 2 3 1 1 1 2
                        1 3 6 7 8 4 5 2 9 0 1 9 2 3 5 4 1 3 8 2 4 9 5 6 7 0 6 7 8 0

ASSOZIATIONSMASS        I I I I I I I I I I I I I I I I I I I I I I I I I I I I I I
                        I I I I I I I I I I I I I I I I I I I I I I I I I I I I I I
          31.00         I I I I I I I I I I I I I -+- I I I I I I I I I I I I I I I
                        I I I I I I I I I I I I I I I I I I I I I I I I I I I I I I
          29.00         I I I -+- I I I I I I I I -+-- I I I I I I I I I I I I I I I
                        I I I   I I I I I I I I     I   I I I I I I I I I I I I I I
          28.00         -+- I   I   I I I I I I     I   I I I I I I I I I I I I I I
                        I I I   I I I I I I I I     I   I I I I I I I I I I I I I I
          26.00         I   -+-- I I I I I I I      I   I -+- I I I I I I I I I I I
                        I   I    I I I I I I I      I   I I   I I I I I I I I I I I
          25.00         I   I    I I I I I I I      I   I I   -+- I I I I I I I I I
                        I   I    I I I I I I I      I   I I   I   I I I I I I I I I
          24.00         --+--    -+- I I I I I      I   I I   I   I I I I I I I I I
                        I        I   I I I I I      I   I I I I   I I I I I I I I I
          22.00         I        I   I I I I I      I   I -+--   I I I I I I I I I
                        I        I   I I I I I      I   I   I    I I I I I I I I I
          20.00         I        I   I I I I I      I   I --+---- I I I I I I I I I
                        I        I   I I I I I      I   I      I  I I I I I I I I I
          19.00         ----+---- I I I I I         I   I      I -+- I I I I I I I
                        I         I I I I I         I   I      I  I   I I I I I I I
          18.00         I         I I I I I         I   I ---+---    I   I I I I I I
                        I         I I I I I         I   I    I       I   I I I I I I
          17.00         I         I -+- -+-         I   I    I       I   I I I I I I
                        I         I I   I           I   I    I       I   I I I I I I
          16.00         I         I I   I           I   I    I       I   I I I I -+-
                        I         I I   I           I   I    I       I   I I I I I
          15.00         ---+----  I     I           I   I    I       I   I I I I I
                        I         I     I           I   I    I       I   I I I I I
          14.00         I         I     I           I   I    I       I   I I I -+-
                        I         I     I           I   I    I       I   I I I I
          13.00         I         I     I           I   I ---+---    I I I   I
                        I         I     I           I   I   I        I I I   I
          12.00         ---+----  I     I           I   I   I        I I I   I
                        I         I     I           I   I   I        I I I   I
           8.00         I         --+---            I   I ---+---   I I   I
                        I               I           I   I   I       I I   I
           4.00         I               I           -------+-------     I I   I
                        I               I                               I I   I
           2.00         I               I           ------+--------       I   I
                        I               I                  I             I   I
           1.00         I               I                  I             --+--
                        I               I                  I             I
           0.00         ----------------------------------+-----------------------
                                                          I
```

Figure 10.12. Maximum solution of the hierarchical cluster analysis of the second control study.

labeled factory by 8 of them. Picture 30, which was not recognized by 12 of the children, received assorted names, such as house (5 times) and school (twice). Picture 27 was called a house 15 times and a school 8 times.

   The fourth cluster consists of four pictures only. They seem to represent a "rest of" category containing those pictures for which the building type had not been well recognized. The picture numbered 16 in Figure 10.11 was called a factory by 14 children and a church by 5 of them. Picture 17 was labeled factory (5 times), school (7 times), and high-rise building (4 times). Picture 18 was not recognized by 10 children, and 9 called it a factory and 5 a church. Picture 20 received the label factory 11 times and was not recognized 4 times.

Comparing the Clusters of Both Control Studies

To facilitate the comparison of the dendrograms resulting from the hierarchical cluster analyses of both control studies, they are shown together in Figure 10.13.

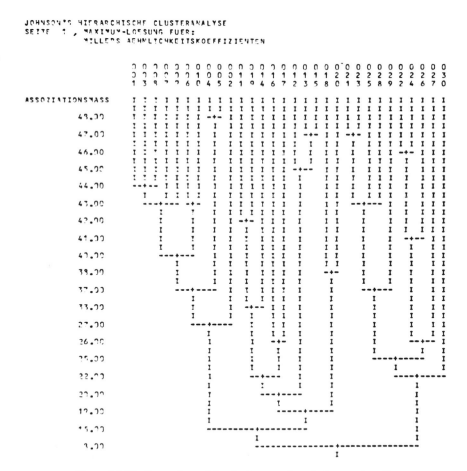

Figure 10.13. Comparison of the dendrograms from both control studies.

```
JOHNSON'S HIERARCHISCHE CLUSTERANALYSE
SEITE   2 , MAXIMUM-LOESUNG FUER:
        SORT.ARCH.KINDER

                        0 0 0 0 0 0 0 0 0 0 0 0 0 0 0 0 0 0 0 0 0 0 0 0 0 0 0 0 0
                        0 0 0 0 0 0 0 0 0 1 1 1 1 1 1 2 2 2 2 2 2 2 2 3 1 1 1 2
                        1 3 6 7 8 4 5 2 9 0 1 9 2 3 5 4 1 3 8 2 4 9 5 6 7 0 6 7 8 0
ASSOZIATIONSMASS        I I I I I I I I I I I I I I I I I I I I I I I I I I I I I
                        I I I I I I I I I I I I I I I I I I I I I I I I I I I I I I
      31.00             I I I I I I I I I I I I -+- I I I I I I I I I I I I I I I
                        I I I I I I I I I I I I I  I I I I I I I I I I I I I I I I
      29.00             I I I -+- I I I I I I  -+-- I I I I I I I I I I I I I I I
                        I I I  I  I I I I I I I  I   I I I I I I I I I I I I I I I
      28.00             -+- I  I  I I I I I I I  I   I I I I I I I I I I I I I I I
                        I  I  I  I I I I I I I  I   I I I I I I I I I I I I I I I
      26.00             I  -+--  I I I I I I I  I   I -+- I I I I I I I I I I I I
                        I   I   I I I I I I I  I   I I  I I I I I I I I I I I I
      25.00             I   I   I I I I I I I  I   I I  -+- I I I I I I I I I I
                        I   I   I I I I I I I  I   I I  I   I I I I I I I I I I
      24.00             --+--   -+- I I I I I  I   I I  I   I I I I I I I I I I
                        I       I I I I I I  I   I I I  I   I I I I I I I I I
      22.00             I       I I I I I I  I   I -+-- I   I I I I I I I I I
                        I       I I I I I I  I   I  I   I   I I I I I I I I I
      20.00             I       I I I I I I  I   I --+--- I I I I I I I I I
                        I       I I I I I I  I   I   I   I I I I I I I I I
      19.00             ----+-----I I I I I  I   I   I   -+- I I I I I I I
      18.00             I       I I I I I I  I   I ---+--- I I I I I I I
      17.00             I       I -+- -+-  I   I   I   I I I I I I I
      16.00             I       I I I  I   I   I   I   I I I I I I -+-
      15.00             ---+----- I  I   I   I   I   I I I I I I  I
      14.00             I       I  I   I   I   I   I   I I I -+- I
      13.00             I       I  I   I   I   I   ---+--- I I  I  I
      12.00             ---+----- I   I   I   I   I   I I  I  I
       8.00             I       --+---  I   I   I   ---+--- I I  I
       4.00             I       I   I   --------+--------  I  I I
       2.00             I       I   I   I   I   ------+------- I I
       1.00             I       I   I   I   I   I   I  --+--
       0.00             -----------------------+--------------------
                                            I
```

Figure 10.13. (*cont.*)

The measure at the left side of the dendrograms indicates the number of subjects who had paired two pictures in one of their groupings and is therefore called "measure of association." The association measure determines whether three, four, five, or more branches or clusters of a dendrogram results.

In this comparison, it can be shown that a solution with five branches for both dendrograms yields the best agreement between the two studies. To obtain a five-cluster solution for the first control study, the dendrogram had to be cut between association measures 20 and 22. For the second control study, the cut had to be between association measures 1 and 2. Now, looking at Figure 10.13 and comparing the first of the five clusters of both control studies, we find that they contain exactly the same pictures. They are the ones with large vertical building shapes and many windows, which most of the children labeled high-rise building.

The fifth cluster of the first control study corresponds to the third cluster of the second study except for the excess of the picture numbered 14 in the dendrogram. Both clusters contain the small horizontal building shapes with few windows most often taken for houses by the children of both studies.

Picture 14, which in the second study is incorporated with the houses in cluster 3, is found in cluster 2 of the first study. This picture was sometimes labeled church and sometimes factory in the first study. In the second study, it was often not recognized at all, or it was held by some children to be a factory.

Cluster 3 of the first control study is contained in cluster 2 of the second one, which in addition holds pictures 11 and 19. These two pictures are part of cluster 2 in the first control study. They are recognized either as churches or as factories. But the three pictures forming cluster 3 in control study 1, and contained in cluster 2 of the second study (i.e., pictures 12, 13, and 15), were definitely labeled churches by the majority of the children.

Building pictures 16 and 17 in the second cluster of control study 1 form cluster 4 in the second control study. They are also two pictures that were not well recognized by the children, picture 16 being sometimes called a factory and picture 17 obtaining many different denominations.

The degree of similarity between the two dendrograms can also be indexed according to the Rand criterion (1971). The similarity measure for the two partitions, namely, .966, is very high. The null hypothesis that there is no difference between the results of the two control studies cannot be rejected. The sorting procedure and the naming of the building types are equivalent methods of recognition.

Both, in turn, do not present results that are critically different from those obtained by the production method, that is, having children draw the building types. Thus the methodological position of the central study of this book is sound.

The Role of Context in Sign Interpretation

I now turn to the second potential criticism that could be leveled against the central study of this book. It has to do with the role of context in the interpretation of signs. A growing criticism of structuralism can be noted recently in the field of semiotics. Among other polemics, this has taken on the form of playing out Peirce against de Saussure, and a rising preoccupation with pragmatism and the semiotic discipline of pragmatics (Morris, 1969). This new tide has shifted the attention of students away from the problem of sign systems as semiotic structures (Prieto, 1975). It is focused instead on interpretation, on the actual coding and decoding of messages in the concrete situation. As was soon noticed, vocabulary and syntax were not sufficient to account for successful encoding or decoding of messages. The communication situation itself—the context in which the message was encoded or decoded—was said to play a decisive role in removing ambiguity in the meaning of a message.

But, unfortunately, the term *context* is not clear. It can be understood in many senses, embracing the span from the actual and virtual paradigmatic position of a sign among other signs to the individual situational, social, and cultural presuppositions entering any communication situation.

However, from the context-bound viewpoint of meaning, the present investigation could be accused of taking a naive—because context-free—stance. Building types, so the argument would run, are never experienced as such but occur always in an urban context. To give children the task of drawing a building type by itself would yield only artificial results.

If this argument was advanced against context-free investigations as such, it would fail on the grounds that there is no study imaginable that would be context free. For instance, the context of the present investigation is inevitably that of the nursery or elementary school's classrooms, with many children who are all instructed to work on the same task—namely, to draw six building types on a sheet of paper subdivided into six fields.

If the argument was against the relevance of the results stemming from this particular experimental context, I would have to return to the beginning of the book where I referred to the theory on which this investigation is based. The context of children's drawings does not only lie in the situation in which they are made. The more important context of children's drawings is mental (or cognitive) and, in addition, remotely environmental. Thus, if a child draws a house, a mosque, or a church, with increasing age the drawings begin to approximate what could be called "stereotypes." These stereotypes are less a result of situational context than of experience. They stem from the way in which children cope with objects like buildings by walking round them, hearing people talk about them, seeing pictures in books or on television of them, etc. This past experience is the main context of the stereotyped images in children's minds. It is past experience which has sharpened some and leveled other features of these images.

The relevance of this investigation lies therefore in the demonstration of how building stereotypes develop in the minds of children by gradual differentiation due to age and environmental context. A further point of importance should be seen in the fact that the building stereotypes are not equally sharpened for all building types. This points at a deficiency in children's context of experience that is not "their fault" but has its origin in a vaguely designed environmental context. If, in an environment, office buildings cannot be distinguished from a high-rise apartment building, and if schools cannot be told apart from offices, children are deprived of distinctive experiences with these buildings. Only vague stereotypes develop in their minds and are then reflected in their drawings. In conclusion, children's drawings of buildings could be used as indicators of vagueness or indistinctiveness in the design of the environmental context in which they live.

In general, however, with respect to semiotic theory, and in particular regarding the main study of this book, context is only one of three aspects or levels of the general principle of semiotic structure.

The lowest level of semiotic structure is given by the mere foregrounding of a sign. If a sign detaches itself as a figure from the ground, the minimal meaning inevitably transmitted by it is the presence of some kind of information (whether or not this is intentionally produced, and whether or not the message is understood). In our study, such information is provided when the first building images emerge from scribbles. Mind you, scribbles are also meaningful, in that they are indices of sensorimotor intelligence. A further level of semiotic structure is attained with syntactic information. Oppositions of gender in language, for instance, permit the receiver of a verbal message to reduce the search for the meaning of words. By gender marking it can be established that the word belongs to the feminine, masculine, or neutral pool of words, and thus, the receiver of the message can reduce the search for meaning by two-thirds of the dictionary. Likewise, the opposition of large versus small or horizontal versus vertical in building shapes permits us to reduce the search for the identification of a building function by one-half (or one-fourth), as in a game of 20 questions.

It is only on the third and last (albeit important) level of semiotic structure that context plays a role. There are contexts that may or may not favor the decoding of the intended meaning of a message. Thus, daylight or darkness favor the correct decoding of the pointers on the wristwatch coded with 12 numerals only (Prieto, 1975). The Turkish flag placed in the context of a building drawing made by a Turkish child clearly indicates that the building is a school. Without this addition, it could have belonged to the smaller, vertically shaped buildings that, because of their size, were not apartment buildings, but—for instance— larger houses.

Some Conclusions

Whereas a certain relevance in the study of distinctive building features lies in using children's drawings as indicators of vagueness or distinctiveness in the design of the environmental context, the relevance of the developmental aspects in this study lies in another direction.

First, it has been shown that the basis of drawing ability is alike across widely differing cultures. This is a strong argument against any form of cultural prejudice.

Second, it becomes clear from this book that it is possible to head-start drawing development, or, in the case of the disabled children, to train their ability to symmetrize graphemes.

If the basis of drawing ability—as the present study shows—is the acquisition of perceptual and motor skills by maturation, the question arises of how this process of maturation could be sustained or, if necessary, accelerated with training. Lurçat (1979) recommends the application of (external) models for pedagogical purposes. She mentions three types of models that may be used with different potentials for success to support the development of drawing ability. The first might be defined as a ''kinesthetic model'' and consists in the adult's hand guiding the hand movement of the child. The second is called a ''visual-kinetic model''; it is produced by the trainer by exhibiting the process of drawing a form and showing children how the traces on paper or on the blackboard grow during drawing. The third is a ''visual-static model'' consisting of the presentation of a finished form (on paper or on the blackboard). Lurçat (1979) argued that the kinesthetic model is optimal since it contains information on form and movement direction. It is therefore especially apt to facilitate the transition from movement (e.g., scribbling) to form, which is typical of the earlier phase of graphic development. It would also seem to be especially capable of compensating for the deficit of symmetry in physically handicapped children.

Whereas kinesthetic models are especially useful in the process of grapheme or form learning, the visual-kinetic model, offering only visual information, functions well in learning directional characteristics in the later phases of graphic development: After form is mastered, the transition from form to direction must be learned, especially in writing, where reversals in direction tend to persist. The much used visual-static model does not appear to have any particular merit in early graphic education.

While advocating the use of the two efficient models each in the right moment of development, Lurçat nevertheless emphasizes the limits of pedagogical intervention and insists on the importance of self-induced graphic exercising and playing for which the educator can only provide the material, the occasion, and at times perhaps, motivational encouragement.

References

Abercrombie, M. L. J. (1964). The disordered body image in cerebral palsy: A questioning look at the concept. *Developmental Medical Child Neurology, 6,* 643–644.

Abercrombie, M. L. J., & Tyson, M. C. (1966). Body image and Draw-a-Man test in cerebral palsy. *Developmental Medical Child Neurology, 8,* 9–15.

Baldwin, J. M. (1895). *Mental development in the child and the race.* New York: MacMillan.

Barnes, E. (1893). A study of children's drawings. *Pedagogical Seminary, 2,* 455–463.

Barnes, E. (1894). The art of little children. (Preface to the condensed English translation of C. Ricci, 1887, *L'arte dei bambini.* Bologna: Zanichelli). *Pedagogical Seminary, 3,* 302.

Barnes, E. (Ed.). (1897). *Studies in education* (Vol. 1). Stanford, CA: Stanford University Press.

Barrett, M. D., & Light, P. H. (1976). Symbolism and intellectual realism in children's drawings. *British Journal of Educational Psychology, 46,* 198–202.

Bassett, E. (1977). Production strategies in the child's drawing of the human figure: Towards an argument for a model of syncretic perception. In Butterworth, G. (Ed.), *The child's representation of the world* (pp. 49–59). New York and London: Plenum.

Baylor, G. W. (1972). A treatise on the mind's eye: An empirical investigation of visual mental imagery. (Doctoral dissertation, Carnegie-Mellon University). Ann Arbor, MI: University Microfilms, No. 72–12.

Bayraktar, R. (1985). Cross-cultural analysis of drawing errors. In N. H. Freeman and M. V. Cox (Eds.), *Visual order.* Cambridge: Cambridge University Press, 333–355.

Brown, E. E. (Ed.). (1897). *Notes on children's drawings.* University of California Studies. Berkeley: University of California, 2–75 (with contributions by M. W. Shinn, K. W. Slack, E. G. Sharp, L. M. Chapman).

Brucker, P. (1982). *Vergleichende Untersuchung von Zeichnungen körperbehinderter und nicht körperbehinderter Kinder.* Erziehungswissenschaftliche Arbeit, erste Staatsprüfung für das Lehramt an Sonderschulen, Fachbereich Sonderpädagogik, PH Reutlingen in Verbindung mit der Universität Tübingen. Unpublished.

Bruner, J. S. (1966). On cognitive growth, I and II. In J. S. Bruner, R. R. Oliver, P. M. Greenfield, *et al.* (Eds.), *Studies in cognitive growth* (pp. 1–67). New York, London, Sidney: John Wiley & Sons.

Bühler, K. (1918). *Die geistige Entwicklung des Kindes.* Jena: Gustav Fischer.

Bühler, K. (1932). *The mental development of the child.* London: Routledge & Kegan Paul.

Buck, J. N. (1974). *The House-Tree-Person (H-T-P) manual supplement*. Los Angeles: Western Psychological Services.

Burk, F. (1902). Genetic versus logical order in drawings. *Pedagogical Seminary, 9,* 296–323.

Burt, C. L. (1921). *Mental and scholastic tests*. London: P. S. King & Son.

Centers, L., & Centers, R. (1963). A comparison of the body images of amputee and non-amputee children as revealed in figure drawings. *Journal of Projective Techniques and Personal Assessment, 27,* 158–165.

Chen, M. J. (1985). Young children's representational drawings of solid objects: A comparison of drawing and copying. In N. H. Freeman and M. V. Cox (Eds.), *Visual order*. Cambridge: Cambridge University Press, 157–175.

Clark, A. B. (1897). The child's attitude towards perspective problems. In E. Barnes (Ed.), *Studies in education* (Vol. 1, pp. 283–294). Stanford, CA: Stanford University Press.

Cooke, E. (1885–1886). Art teaching and child nature. *London Journal of Education, 1885,* 465, 1,886, 12.

Denis, W. (1958). Handwriting conventions as determinants of human figure drawings. *Journal of Consulting Psychology, 22,* 293–295.

Dilley, M. G., & Paivio, A. (1968). Pictures and words as stimulus and response items in paired-associate learning of young children. *Journal of Experimental Child Psychology, 6,* 231–240.

Eng, H. (1931). *The psychology of children's drawings*. London: Routledge and Kegan Paul.

Frances, S. (1953). Recherches sur la perspective dans les dessins d'enfants. *Bulletin de Psychologie, 6–7,* 419–424.

Freeman, N. H. (1972). Process and product in children's drawings. *Perception, 1,* 123–140.

Freeman, N. H. (1980). *Strategies of representation in young children: Analysis of spatial skills and drawing processes*. New York: Academic Press.

Freeman, N. H., & Cox, M. V. (Eds.). (1985). *Visual order*. Cambridge: Cambridge University Press.

Gallagher, M. (1897). Children's spontaneous drawings. *Northwestern Monthly* (Lincoln, NE), *8,* 130–134.

Gesell, A. (1925). *The mental growth of the pre-school child*. New York: MacMillan.

Golomb, C. (1973). Children's representation of the human figure: The effects of models, media, and instruction. *Genetic Psychology Monographs, 87,* 197–251.

Golomb, C. (1974). *Young children's sculpture and drawing*. Cambridge, MA: Harvard University Press.

Golomb, C. (1977). Representational development of the human figure: A look at the neglected variables of SES, IQ, sex, and verbalization. *The Journal of Genetic Psychology, 131,* 207–222.

Golomb, C., & Barr-Grossman, T. (1977). Representational development of the human figure in familial retardates. *Genetic Psychology Monographs, 95,* 247–266.

Golomb, C., & Farmer, D. (1983). Children's graphic planning strategies and early principles of spatial organization in drawing. *Studies in Art Education 24/2,* 86–100.

Gombrich, E. (1969). *Art and illusion: A study in the psychology of pictorial representation*. Princeton, NJ: Princeton University Press.

Goodenough, F. L. (1926). *Measurement of intelligence by drawing*. Yonkers, NY: World Book.

Goodenough, F. L. (1928). Studies in the psychology of children's drawings. *Psychological Bulletin, 25,* 272–283.

Goodenough, F. L., & Harris, D. B. (1950). Studies in the psychology of children's drawings: II. 1928–1949. *Psychological Bulletin, 47* (5), 369–433.

Goodnow, J. (1977). *Children's drawing*. London: Open Books.

Götze, C. (1898). *Das Kind als Künstler*. Hamburg: Boysen & Maasch.

Graewe, H. (1936). Geschichtlicher Überblick über die Psychologie des kindlichen Zeichnens. *Archiv der gesamten Psychologie, 96,* 103–220.

Graewe, H. (1935). Das Tierzeichnen der Kinder. Zeitschrift für pädagogische Psychologie, *36*, 251–300.

Gridley, P. F. (1939). Graphic representation of a man by four-year-old children in nine prescribed drawing situations. *Genetic Psychology Monographs, 20,* 183–350.

Hagen, M. A. (1985). There is no development in art. In N. H. Freeman and M. V. Cox (Eds.), *Visual order.* Cambridge: Cambridge University Press, 59–77.

Hall, G. S. (1892a). The contents of children's mind on entering school. *Pedagogical Seminary, 1,* 139–173, especially 165–166 (originally published in 1882).

Hall, G. S. (1892b). Notes on children's drawings. Literature and notes. *Pedagogical Seminary, 1,* 445–447.

Hammer, E. F. (1964). *The House-Tree-Person (H-T-P) clinical research manual.* Los Angeles: Western Psychological Services.

Hancock, J. A. (1894). A preliminary study of motor ability. *Pedagogical Seminary, 3,* 9–29.

Harris, D. B. (1963). *Children's drawings as measures of intellectual maturity. A revision and extension of the Goodenough Draw-a-Man Test.* New York: Harcourt, Brace & World.

Herrick, M. A. (1894). Children's drawings. *Pedagogical Seminary, 3,* 338–339.

Hicks, M. D. (1893). Art in early education. *Pedagogical Seminary, 2,* 463–466.

Hogan, L. E. (1898). *A study of a child.* London, New York: Harper & Brothers.

Hoyt, C. (1941). Test reliability obtained by analysis of variance. *Psychometrica, 6,* 153–160.

Ivanoff, E. (1909). Recherches experimentales sur le dessin des ecoliers de la Suisse Romande. *Archives de Psychologie, 8,* 97–156.

Johnson, S. C. (1967). Hierarchical clustering schemes. *Psychometrica, 32* (3), 241–254.

Kalyan-Masih, V. (1976). Graphic representation: From intellectual realism to visual realism in Draw-a-House-Tree task. *Child Development, 47,* 1026–1031.

Kerr, M. (1937). Children's drawings of houses. *British Journal of Medical Psychology, 16,* 206–218.

Kerschensteiner, G. (1905). *Die Entwicklung der zeichnerischen Begabung.* München: Carl Gerber.

Kosslyn, S. M., Heldmeyer, K. H., & Locklear, E. L. (1977). Children's drawings as data about internal representations. *Journal of Experimental Child Psychology, 23,* 191–211.

Krampen, M. (1979). *Meaning in the urban environment.* London: Pion.

Krampen, M. (1981). The developmental semiotics of Jean Piaget (1896–1980). *Semiotica, 34–3/4,* 193–218.

Krampen, M. (1986a). Developmental semiotics. In *Encyclopedic Dictionary of Semiotics* (pp. 190–196). Berlin, New York, Amsterdam: Mouton de Gruyter.

Krampen, M. (1986b). The development of children's drawings as a phase in the ontogeny of iconicity. In P. Bouissac, M. Herzfeld, & R. Posner (Eds.), *Iconicity. Essays on the nature of culture* (pp. 141–191). Tübingen: Stauffenburg Verlag.

Krampen, M., Espe, H., Öztürk, K., Ertürk, S., Özbilen, A., & Saltik, H. (1980). *Turkish children's drawings of different building types.* Research Report. UNDP/UNESCO Project TUR/75/012, mimeographed.

Laszlo, J. I., & Broderick, P. A. (1985). The perceptual-motor skill of drawing. In N. H. Freeman and M. V. Cox (Eds.), *Visual order.* Cambridge: Cambridge University Press, 356–373.

Leontiev, A. N., & Gippenreiter, Y. B. (1966). Concerning the activity of man's visual system. In *Psycholgocial Research in the USSR* (pp. 361–392). Moscow: Progress Publishers.

Levinstein, S. (1905). *Kinderzeichnungen bis zum 14. Lebensjahr.* Leipzig: R. Voigtländer.

Lukens, H. T. (1897). A study of children's drawings in the early years. *Pedagogical Seminary, 4,* 79–109.

Luquet, G. H. (1912). Le premier age du dessin enfantin. *Archives de psychologie, 12,* 14–20.

Luquet, G. H. (1913). *Les dessins d'un enfant.* Paris: Alcan.

Luquet, G. H. (1922a). La methode dans l'étude des dessins d'enfants. *Journal de Psychologie, 19,* 193–221.

Luquet, G. H. (1922b). Genèse de l'art figuré. *Journal de Psychologie, 19,* 695–719.

Luquet, G. H. (1924). L'étude statistique des dessins d'enfants. *Journal de Psychologie,* 738–756.

Luquet, G. H. (1927). *Le dessin enfantin.* Paris: Alcan.

Lurçat, L. (1972–1973). Luquet et le dessin de l'enfant. *Bulletin de Psychologie, 12–13,* 698–700.

Lurçat, L. (1979). *L'activité graphique à l'école maternelle.* Paris: Les Editions ESF.

Machover, K. (1949). *Personality projection in the drawing of the human figure.* Springfield, IL: Thomas.

Machover, K. (1953). Human figure drawings of children. *Journal of Projective Techniques, 17,* 85–91.

Maitland, L. (1895, September 1). What children draw to please themselves. *Inland Educator* (Terre Haute, IN), pp. 77–81.

Maitland, L. (1899). Notes on Eskimo drawings. *Northwestern Monthly* (Lincoln, NE), *9,* 443–450.

Markham, S. (1954). An item analysis of children's drawings of a house. *Journal of Clinical Psychology, 10,* 185–187.

Martin, W. E., & Damrin, D. E. (1951). An analysis of the reliability and factorial composition of ratings of children's drawings. *Child Development, 22,* 133–144.

McDermott, L. (1897). Favourite drawings of Indian children. *Northwestern Monthly* (Lincoln, NE), *8,* 134–137.

Meili-Dworetzki, G. (1957). *Das Bild des Menschen in der Vorstellung und Darstellung des Kleinkindes.* Bern: Hans Huber.

Miller, G. A. (1969). A psychological method to investigate verbal concepts. *Journal of Mathematical Psychology, 6,* 169–191.

Morris, C. (1964). *Signification and significance: A study of the relations of signs and values.* Cambridge, MA: M.I.T. Press.

Morris, C. R. (1969). *Signs, language and behavior.* New York: Prentice Hall.

Morris, D. (1962). *The biology of art.* London: Methuen.

Muchow, M. (1925). Pädagogisch-psychologische und entwicklungspsychologische Betrachtungsweise in der Psychologie der Kindheit. *Zeitschrift für pädagogische Psychologie, 26,* 316–321, 346–352.

Norman, D. A., & Rumelhart, D. F. (1975). *Explorations in cognition.* San Francisco: W. H. Freeman.

Olivier, F. (1974). Le dessin enfantin est-il une écriture? *Enfance, 3–5,* 183–216.

Osgood, C. E. (1958). *Method and theory in experimental psychology.* New York: Oxford University Press.

O'Shea, M. V. (1894). A study on drawings of children in the schools of Winnoa, Minn., by children from five to seventeen years. *Proceedings of the National Education Association,* 1015–1023.

O'Shea, M. V. (1897). Some aspects of drawing. *Educational Review, 14,* 263–284.

Paine, R. S. (1964). The concept of body image and extracorporeal space as revealed in children's drawings. *Developmental Medical Child Neurology, 6,* 643.

Paivio, A. (1969). Mental imagery in associative learning and memory. *Psychological Review, 76,* 241–263.

Paivio, A. (1970). On the functional significance of imagery. *Psychological Bulletin, 73,* 385–392.

Paivio, A., & Csapo, K. (1973). Picture superiority in free recall: Imagery of dual coding? *Cognitive Psychology, 5,* 176–206.

Paivio, A., & Yarmey, A. D. (1966). Pictures versus words as stimuli and responses in paired-associate learning. *Psychonomic Science, 5,* 235–236.

Pappenheim, K. (1899). Bemerkungen über Kinderzeichnungen. *Zeitschrift für pädagogische Psychologie, 1, 2,* 57–73.

Passy, J. (1891). Notes sur les dessins d'enfants. *Revue Philosophique, 32,* 614.

Peirce, C. S. (1965–1966). *Collected papers of Charles Sanders Peirce* (Vol. I–IV). Charles Hartshorne, Paul Weiss, and Arthur W. Burks (Eds.). Cambridge: Harvard University Press.

Perez, M. B. (1888). *L'art et la poésie chez l'enfant*. Paris: Alcan.

Piaget, J. (1922). Pour l'étude des explications d'enfants. *L'educateur, 3*, 33–39.

Piaget, J. (1923a). *Le langage et la pensée chez l'enfant*. Neuchatel and Paris: Delachaux et Niestlé.

Piaget, J. (1923b). La pensée symbolique et la pensée de l'enfant. *Archives de Psychologie, 18*, 208–224.

Piaget, J. (1927). *La causalité physique chez l'enfant*. Paris: Alcan.

Piaget, J. (1963a). *The origins of intelligence in the child* (M. Cook, Trans.). New York: Norton. (Original work published 1936)

Piaget, J. (1963b). *The psychology of intelligence* (M. Piercy and D. E. Berlyne, Trans.). Paterson, NJ: Littlefield, Adams. (Original work published 1947)

Piaget, J. (1971). *Structuralism* (Chaninah Maschler, Trans.). London: Routledge & Kegan Paul. (Original work published 1968)

Piaget, J., & Inhelder, B. (1948). *La représentation de l'espace chez l'enfant*. Paris: Presses Universitaires de France.

Piaget, J., & Inhelder, B. (1966). *L'image mentale chez l'enfant*. Paris: Presses Universitaires de France.

Piaget, J., & Inhelder, B. (1967). *The child's conception of space* (F. J. Langdon and J. L. Lunzer, Trans.). New York: Norton. (Original work published 1948)

Piaget, J., & Inhelder, B., (1969). *The psychology of the child* (H. Weaver, Trans.). New York: Basic Books. (Origfinal work published 1966)

Prieto, L. J. (1975). *Pertinence et pratique*. Paris: Les Editions de Minuit.

Pylyshyn, Z. W. (1973). What the mind's eye tells the mind's brain. A critique of mental imagery. *Psychological Bulletin, 80*, 1–24.

Rand, G. (1972). Children's images of houses: A prologonema to the study of why people still want pitched roofs. In W. J. Mitchell (Ed.), *Environmental Design: Research and Practice, I* (pp. 6-9-1–6-9-10). Los Angeles: University of California Press.

Rand, W. M. (1971). Objective criteria for the evaluation of clustering methods. *Journal of the American Statistics Association, 66*, 846–850.

Ribault, C. (1965). Le dessin de la maison chez l'enfant. *Revue de Neuropsychiatrie Infantile et d'Hygiene Mentale de l'Enfance, 13* (1–2), 83–100.

Ricci, C. (1887). *L'arte dei bambini*. Bologna: Zanichelli.

Ritchey, G. H. (1980). Picture superiority in free recall: The effects of organization and elaboration. *Journal of Experimental Child Psychology, 29*, 460–474.

Rouma, G. (1912). *Le langage graphique de l'enfant*. Bruxelles: Misch & Thron.

Schilder, P. F. (1935). *The image and appearance of the human body*. Psyche Monographs, No. 4. London: Kegan Paul, Trench, Trubner.

Schubert, A. (1930). Drawings of Orotchen children and young people. *Pedagogical Seminary, 37*, 232–243.

Scripture, E. W., & Lyman, C. S. (1892–1893). Drawing a straight line: A study in experimental didactics. *Studies from the Yale Psychological Laboratory 1*, 92.

Sebeok, T. A. (1977). Ecumenicalism in semiotics. In T. A. Sebeok (Ed.), *A perfusion of signs* (pp. 180–206). Bloomington and London: Indiana University Press.

Shinn, M. W. (1893). Notes on the development of a child. *University of California Studies* (Vol. 1, pp. 1–4). Berkeley, CA: University of California.

Siegel, S. (1956). *Nonparametric statistics for the behavioral sciences*. New York: McGraw-Hill.

Silverstein, A. B., & Robinson, H. A. (1956). The representation of orthopedic disability in children's figure drawings. *Journal of Consulting Psychology, 20*, 333–340.

Smythies, J. R. (1935). Experience and description of the human body. *Brain, 76*, 132.

Stern, W. (1908). Sammlungen freier Kinderzeichnungen. *Zeitschrift für angewandte Psychologie und psychologische Sammelforschung, 1*, 179–187.

Stern, W. (1909). Die Entwicklung der Raumwahrnehmung in der ersten Kindheit. *Zeitschrift für angewandte Psychologie und psychologische Sammelforschung, 2,* 412–423.

Stern, C., & Stern, W. (1910). Die zeichnerische Entwicklung eines Knaben vom 4. bis zum 7. Jahre. *Zeitschrift für angewandte Psychologie und psychologische Sammelforschung, 3,* 1–31.

Sully, J. (1896). *Studies of childhood.* New York: D. Appleton.

Tabary, J. C. (1964). Body image and spontaneous geometry of the normal and the cerebral-palsied child. *Developmental Medical Child Neurology, 6,* 643.

Thomas, G. V., & Silk, A. M. J. (1990). *An introduction to the psychology of children's drawings.* New York: Harvester Wheatsheaf.

Tracy, F. (1899). *Psychologie der Kindheit.* Leipzig: Ernst Wunderlich.

Uexküll, J. von (1921). Der Funktionskreis. In *Umwelt und Innenwelt der Tiere* (pp. 44–49). Berlin: Julius Springer.

Vekker, L. M. (1961). Some theoretical problems of the image of touch. In O'Connor, N. (Ed.), *Recent Soviet Psychology* (pp. 131–140). Oxford, London, New York, Paris: Pergamon Press.

Vurpillot, E. (1976). *The visual world of the child.* London: George Allen & Unwin.

Wallon, H., & Lurçat, L. (1957). Graphisme et modèle dans les dessins de l'enfant. *Journal de Psychologie, 3,* 257–278.

Wallon, H., & Lurçat, L. (1958). Le dessin du personage par l'enfant, ses étapes et ses mutations. *Enfance, 3,* 177–211.

Wallon, H., & Lurçat, L. (1959). L'espace graphique de l'enfant. *Journal de Psychologie, 4,* 427–453.

Wekker, L. M. (1966). On the basic properties of the mental image and a general approach to their analogue simulation. In *Psychological Research in the USSR* (pp. 310–333). Moscow: Progress Publishers.

Willats, J. (1985). Drawing systems revisited: The role of denotation systems in children's figure drawings. In N. H. Freeman and M. V. Cox (Eds.), *Visual order.* Cambridge: Cambridge University Press, 78–100.

Williams, J. F. (1964). Body image and children's drawings. *Developmental Medical Child Neurology, 6,* 643.

Wilson, B., & Wilson, M. (1984). Children's drawings in Egypt: Cultural style acquisition as graphic development. *Visual Arts Research, 10* (19), 13–26.

Wysocki, B. A., & Whitney, E. (1965). Body image of crippled children as seen in Draw-a-Person test behavior. *Perceptual and Motor skills, 21,* 499–504.

Wysocki, B. A., & Wysocki, A. C. (1973). The body-image of normal and retarded children. *Journal of Clinical Psychology, 29,* 7–10.

Zaporozhets, A. V. (1965). The development of perception in the preschool child. In P. E. Mussen (Ed.), European research in cognitive development. *Monographs of the Society for Research in Child Development, 39,* Monograph 100, 82–101.

Zaporozhets, A. V., & Zinchenko, V. P. (1966). Development of perceptual activity and formation of a sensory image in the child. In *Psychological Research in the USSR.* (393–421). Moscow: Progress Publishers.

Zinchenko, V. P., van Chizi-Tsin, V., & Tarakanov, V. V. (1963). The formation and development of perceptual activity. *Soviet Psychology and Psychiatry, 1,* 3–12.

Index

Abstract, 23, 57
Afferent information, 44, 120
Age, 9, 38, 87, 90, 94, 96, 123, 133, 134, 146, 149–158, 162, 163, 182–195, 188, 211; *see also* Model parameters, Variables, demographic
Age groups, 67–70, 157, 159, 162, 163, 165, 169, 172, 173, 183, 184, 190, 192, 201
Age levels, 88, 165, 166
Alternation, 65, 66
Alternative hypothesis, 127, 128, 130, 131
Amputee, 94
Analysis of variance, 87, 148, 150, 151, 153, 159, 160, 161, 163, 182, 183, 187
Angular, 101–103
Angular continuous traces, 63, 64
Animals, 34, 35, 39, 51, 54, 58, 75, 77, 122
Apartment building, 103, 107; *see also Building type*
Arabesques, 52, 53, 57
Arbitrary, 18, 19
Architectural, 194, 198
Architectural features, 168, 177, 178, 182
Architectural variables, 182, 191
  forms of roof, 152, 185–187
  number of stories, 152, 185, 186
  number of windows, 152, 185–187
  secondary buildings, 152, 185
  size of building, 152, 183, 184
  size of windows, 152, 183, 184
  verticality/horizontality of buildings, 152, 185

Architectural variables (*cont.*)
  verticality/horizontality of windows, 152, 185, 187
  See also Distinctive architectural features
Asymmetry, 164

Biographic method, 32
Bodily impairment, 92
Body
  concept, 95
  image, 93–95
  scheme, 93, 95
  symmetry, 164
Building
  drawing, v, 75, 77, 86, 96, 147, 148, 160, 161, 164, 167
  function, 76, 104
  feature; *see* Distinctive architectural features
  shapes
    rectangles, 104
    squares, 104
  stereotypes, 148, 222; *see also* Stereotype
  type, v, 4
Building drawing
  apartment building, 78, 86, 204
  church, 3, 76, 89, 205
  factory, 9, 86, 206
  house, 6, 86, 207
  mosque, 96
  office, 9, 86, 203
  religious, 9
  school, 9, 86, 208